IREL

WHERE TO EAT AND STAY ON THE
WILD ATLANTIC WAY

**written and photographed by
John & Sally McKenna**

**with special correspondent
William Barry**

[E] Estragon Press

[E]

First published by in 2014
by Estragon Press Ltd
Durrus, Bantry, County Cork
Text and Photographs © Estragon Press

website www.guides.ie

ISBN 978-1-906927-20-2

Written by John McKenna

Publishing Manager: Sally McKenna
Special correspondent: William Barry
Web: Fluidedge
Digital Editions: Dónal Mulligan
Copy Editor: Judith Casey
Editorial Assistant: Eve Clancy
Printed by Graphycems

Photographic Credits:
Leslie Williams page 86
Matthew Thompson page 87
PJ McKenna pages 78, 114 & 136
all other photos by Sally & John McKenna
Graphic Credits:
Fork by Dmitry Baranovskiy
Moon by Maurizio Fusillo
both from The Noun Project

Acknowledgements:
The publishers would like to thank Frank McKevitt, Edwina Murray, Chris Carroll, Paul Neilan, the Gill & MacMillan team, Hugh Stancliffe and staff at Graphycems.

For Jim Kennedy with thanks.

with special thanks to our team of editors: Eamon Barrett, William Barry, Caroline Byrne, Aoife Cox, Caroline Hennessey, Joe McNamee & Leslie Williams.

Many of the places featured in this book are only open during the summer season, which means that they can be closed for any given length of time between October and March. Booking is always advisable.

We greatly appreciate receiving emails with suggestions and criticisms from readers, and would like to thank those who have written in the past, whose opinions are of enormous assistance to us when considering which people, places and products finally make the *McKennas' Guides*. www.guides.ie

We are on Facebook and Twitter
https://www.facebook.com/
wheretoeatandstayonthewildatlanticway
@McKennasGuides

CONTENTS

The Foyle Bridge, Inishowen & the Fanad Peninsula

In Donegal, in wintertime, the roads and trees unite in their boot-black, bible-black starkness, an ancient bog oak darkness that gives the small fields a feeling of utter, aching loneliness. Driving through the valleys, the roads feel like intrusions into a wild landscape, crawling through animate nature while the mountains maintain a snarlful eye as you run a gauntlet through them, past ferns as torchy red as the young Maureen O'Hara's hair. That lazy wind will rush straight through you and into your bones, should you decide to take a walk on the northern beaches. The light is as cold as that line from TS Eliot's *The Waste Land*: '*I will show you fear in a handful of dust.*'

WILD ATLANTIC WAY

Summer scatters this gloom and introversion, and one then thinks of Eliot again: '*Yet with these April sunsets, that somehow recall/My buried life, and Paris in the Spring/I feel immeasurably at peace, and find the world/To be wonderful and youthful, after all*'.

Nowhere else offers the intense brilliance of a sunset in Donegal, nothing can compete with the lurid volumes of russet and rouge light that anoint the county. The harshness and starkness of winter is repelled, the county is wonderful and youthful , after all.

Guildhall Cafés

Derry's famous 17th century landmark is a centre for social, political and cultural events. There are two brilliant cafés associated with the Guildhall – **Guild,** which is housed in the riverside entrance to the building, and **Legenderry Warehouse No 1**, which is adjacent to the main building. Guild opens onto the riverside selling snacks and drinks prepared by much-loved Bundoran restaurant The Beach House. Legenderry Warehouse is great for brunch and is proud of it's wonderful coffee. It's a funky, don't-miss! place. It also sports a very funky shop with very smart goods to bring home from the maiden city.

Legenderry Warehouse No 1, Guildhall Street, Derry + 44 2871 264798 www. legenderrywarehouseno1. com

Guild, The Guildhall, Derry + 44 2871 360505 www.guildcafe.co.uk

Pyke 'n' Pommes

If you stroll down to Queens Quay, hard by the River Foyle, you will find Pyke 'n' Pommes, and you will have found the food truck of your dreams. You make your mind up, place your order – *The Codfather; the Notorious P.I.G; the Legenderry Burger* – you sit on a bench or you sit in your car and enjoy it, and you ask yourself: how on earth can this food, which has been finished in an old British Leyland truck parked beside a river, possibly be so good? This is restaurant quality food, this is cutting-edge food, this is magnificent food. The sourcing is superlative, and the finishing does more than justice to impeccable ingredients.

"It's a bit of theatre, having a bit of craic. That's what makes it work", says Mr Pyke, but there's more to it than that. What makes it work is Mr Pyke's passionate conviction, as well as his sourcing and his skills. *Queen's Quay, Derry +44 7594 307561 www.pykenpomes.com. Open daily.*

The Merchant House & The Saddler's House

Joan Pyne is a woman in search of an authenticity, in search of an aesthetic. Her restoration work on two major Derry properties – The Saddler's House and The Merchant's House – is valuable and important work, especially in a Province that is often fixated on the historical past, but careless about its architectural heritage. And, the breakfasts are terrific: don't miss the marmalade! *Saddler's House, 36 Gt James Street, Derry; Merchant House, 16 Queen Street, Derry + 44 2871 269691 www.thesaddlershouse.com.*

Browns & Browns in Town

Ian Orr is cooking some of the best food in Ireland right now. Browns delivers some of the most interesting, and involving contemporary cooking that you will find anywhere, yet what is instructive about Ian Orr is that his cooking is not at all didactic. His food is not grandstanding, he cooks for pleasure and comfort, not to show off, or demonstrate what a hot shot he is. It's the same in Brown's in Town, Ian Orr's second restaurant. BIT is indubitably swish, and it's a good swishness because it isn't blowsy or brash: it's subtle and restrained and, thereby, all the better. It's the kind of room that makes you want to party, the kind of restaurant that shouts: restaurant! You might find yourself settling into one of those gorgeous booths and find, suddenly, that it is several hours later.

The cooking is red hot, modern and unselfconscious, and the team deliver it with polished perfection. *1 Bonds Hill + 44 2871 345180; 23 Strand Road + 44 2871 362889 www.brownsrestaurant.com. Open lunch and dinner.*

Above: Legenderry Warehouse No 1

Below: The Merchant House in the Georgian district and Pyke'n'Pommes food truck.

The Custom House

This gorgeous restaurant and wine bar looks like something straight out of central Manhattan, and its restoration has been beautifully and painstakingly achieved. Christopher Moran's menus offer an extensive tableau of dishes, all centred on properly curated foods – sourcing fish from Greencastle, 21-day aged steaks from Antrim, and chicken from Armagh, and there are lots of tasty things to tempt the appetite: crispy hen's egg with streaky bacon and homemade brown sauce; chef's lamb plate with aubergine caviar; cod with spinach and fennel potato. Stylish and very professional. *Custom House St, Queens Quay, Derry + 44 2871 373366 www.customhouserestaurant. com. Open lunch and dinner.*

Local Food

Northern Ireland is famous for its "Home Bakeries". Be sure to ask for the local Northern Irish breads for breakfast: these include *fadge* (potato bread) and *farls* (a quick-rising soda bread, made from either white or brown flour).

Local Food

Look out for the artisan breads baked by the **SlowFoodCo.** These are genuinely slow cooked in a wood-fired pizza oven. You can find them in Harry's, including the Saturday market, and The Counter and other outlets.

www.slowfood-co.com
+ 44 7793 917877 or
+ 353 74 915 6777

Harry's Saturday Market

Nothing can start your journey off along the Wild Atlantic Way better than a visit to the Saturday market at Harry's Restaurant. You'll find SlowFoodCo breads and cakes. There are splendid vegetarian pies and treats. There is the most wonderful goat meat. There is artisan pork and beef and bacon and sausage. There is the most amazing fish and shellfish from Greencastle. There are fabulous vegetables from Harry's own walled garden. In short, there is everything you need if you are preparing a picnic for the journey. And then, shopping finished, it's straight into Harry's for some delicious brunchy, zappy, tasty food and ace coffees to get the motor running. And do try this: hot Hamilton's Farm pork sausage; fresh cold Greencastle oyster, then a sip of Kinnegar ale. Ah!
Bonemaine, Bridgend, County Donegal + 353 74 936 8544 www.harrys.ie. Market open Sat morning.

Harry's Restaurant

Donal Doherty isn't a man to stand still. Having built the weekend market at Harry's into a whizz-bang success with a brilliant array of producers – Slow Food Co sourdough breads; Carlan Foods sweet things; Hamilton Farm rare-breed pork; Donegal shellfish; Greencastle fish; Dexter beef from Marshalls; McArthur's lamb; Dermot Carey's organic vegetables – 2014 has also seen the arrival of the brilliant Derek Creagh as head chef, and there will be a new food offering in a re-built bar area which will feature a meat hanging room, and probably a roving food operation touring the coastal towns of the county.

So, as ever, it's all go at Harry's, and the signature style of Inishowen ingredients on an Inishowen menu produces superlative foods with superlative tastes – Greencastle queen scallops with garlic flowers and romanesco from the walled garden; mackerel ceviche with beet aioli; pork belly with pea tendrils and onion confit; trio of Dexter beef (sirloin; tenderloin; and rump) with broccoli rabe and dauphinoise potatoes; panna cotta with raspberry sorbet. The tastes and textures are vivid, bracing and beautiful, and Mr Doherty is the best host. *Bonemaine, Bridgend, County Donegal + 353 74 936 8544 www.harrys.ie. Open lunch in dinner, brunch weekends.*

Kealy's Seafood Bar

Kealy's of Greencastle has always been a restaurant where seafood is treated with classical respect and restraint – haddock with a Stilton sauce; salmon with bearnaise sauce; john dory with anchovy butter; dover sole meuniere; lobster thermidor. These dishes are as unchanging, timeless and confident as is Kealy's itself, one of the country's classic seafood restaurants. If for some reason you don't want to try the fish, they source excellent Angus beef from Mullan's organic farm in 'Derry, and have some nice vegetarian choices. *The Harbour, Greencastle, County Donegal + 353 74 938 1010 www.kealysseafoodbar. ie. Open lunch and dinner.*

Opposite: Brunch on Harry's Market day.

Below: Harry's Restaurant and Saturday market.

McGrory's

The Inishowen legend that is the mighty McGrory's powers on, with siblings Anne, John and Neil ladling out the hospitality as to the Donegal manner born. There is something that is so very generous about this trio as they go about their business: managing the bar, managing the restaurant and the rooms, managing the music and the gigs, that it animates the entire place. The music sessions held here in Culdaff are the stuff of legend, of course – Townes van Zandt live! – but McGrory's is special whether you can pick with a plectrum or pluck a pizzicato, or whether your speciality is listening to other people doing just that. Creating a destination address in such a remote, northerly place is an heroic act, and the McGrorys exude the culture of their area with delightful charm. *Culdaff, County Donegal + 353 74 937 9104 www.mcgrorys.ie. Open lunch and dinner.*

Caffe Banba

Dominic and Andrea aren't just the most Northerly baristas in Ireland, they are also surely the bravest. For when the wind whips around Banba's Head up there at Malin Head, at the most northerly extremity of Ireland, it is a fearsome proposition to even be brave enough to get out of the car. But summon up your courage and head over for a beautiful coffee and some lovely buns and cakes, all sold from the Banba coffee bar on wheels. There is also a Caffe Banba shop in Carndonagh where you can secure that vital hit of good caffeine in more sedate surroundings. *Ballyhillion, Malin Head, County Donegal + 353 74 937 0538 www.caffebanba.com – Open daily during the summer months.*

Done

There are six off the coast of Donegal, of which **Island** is the best known. All the island reachable by ferry boat with **Oileán Ruaidh** approachable by car at low tide. All beautiful places to bring a picnic – and a raincoat!

www.donegalislands.com

Below: Caffe Banba at Malin Head.

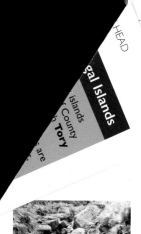

Claire The Bakers

Claire's is a little husband-and-wife-run café in the SuperValu shopping centre at Carndonagh. A great place to buy a picnic, or to stop by for coffee and a sandwich. Home-made cakes are their real speciality. *Unit ... uperValu, Carndonagh, County Donegal + 353 74 ... / 3927. Open daily Mon-Sat.*

The Glen House

When *The Irish Times* travel writer Fionn Davenport picked his favourite place to rest his head in the Northwest for the "Defining Ireland" series, the place he chose was Sonia McGonagle's The Glen House, in little Clonmany. We understand perfectly. Mrs McGonagle is one of the most meticulous hostesses, with an obsessive attention to detail, whether it is the correct way to place sandwiches and buns on a cake tier, or how to dress a room, or the standard of housekeeping that makes everyone happy. The Glen pushes all the buttons, therefore, and we can't think of anything nicer than a few days here spent walking on the beaches and on through the Urris Hills and the Mamore Gap, with the promise of dinner in The Glen to end a perfect day. *Straid, Clonmany, County Donegal + 353 74 937 6745 www.glenhouse.ie.*

The Beach House Bar & Restaurant

Claire McGowan is a great restaurateur, and The Beach House is a great Buncrana restaurant. It is great because it feels right, because the food feels right, because the room seems to act almost like a tabula rasa: ready to be whatever you want it to be, whether that is a bowl of soup and a sandwich at lunchtime or a blowout special with a bunch of friends. We can explain this effect by saying simply that Ms McGowan's focus is entirely on her customers – she is one of the new generation of hosts who are transforming the reputation of Donegal. The cooking is right on the money: a tasting plate of local crab; deep-fried St Tola's goat's cheese and beetroot ice cream; Greencastle cod with freshwater prawns; Donegal fillet steak with red wine jus; Beach House snowball. The wine list is superb, service is understated and polite, and value for money is excellent. Ms McGowan also runs Guild café at the Guildhall in Derry. *Swilly Road, Buncrana, County Donegal + 353 74 936 1050 www.thebeachhouse.ie. Open lunch and dinner.*

The Red Door

Sean Clifford has charge of the kitchens in The Red Door in Fahan, a gorgeous house with the most gorgeous location on the water's edge. It's a hugely popular wedding destination, but there are also rooms for regular guests. It's a great spot for afernoon tea, and Mr Clifford's cooking is imaginative and creative – Donegal beef with Muckish red ale and blue cheese rarebit; hake on the bone with lobster cream; pork belly with crispy pork shoulder. *Fahan, Inishowen, County Donegal + 353 74 936 0289 www.thereddoor.ie. Open lunch and dinner.*

Local Food

Philip and Sarah Moss have run Filligan's, one of the most distinctive and creative artisan food businesses in Ireland, for almost twenty years now. **Filligan's Preserves** are available locally in good B&Bs and shops, and they just have to be on your shopping list. *Sarah & Philip Moss, Tullyard, Glenties, County Donegal + 353 74 955 1628 www.filligans.com*

Above: Richard Finney
Below: The Counter

The Counter

Richard Finney is a man who makes things happen, and in The Counter he has created a classy wine shop, one that takes the wine shop concept into new territory for Donegal. Sure, you can come in with nothing but a bottle of Pinot Grigio on your mind, but the chances are that you will leave with the Pinot Grigio, and with some Ballinasloe goat's cheese, and wood-oven baked breads from The Slow Food Co., and a slice of roasted cauliflower and mascarpone tart, and a bar of Skelligs chocolate and some Gaeta olives and a cup of Badger & Dodo and a couple of bottles of Donegal craft beer... Phew! Got all that? The Counter has all you need as well as fantastic wines, and Mr Finney is a serious player in Donegal's food culture, a man who makes things happen. *Canal Road, Letterkenny, County Donegal + 353 74 9120075 www.thecounter-deli.com. Open daily.*

Rathmullan House

For more than fifty years, the Wheeler family have welcomed guests to their gorgeous country house, Rathmullan House, on the shores of Lough Swilly, on the edge of Rathmullan village. The achievement of Bob and Robin Wheeler, and their sons Mark and William, is simply immense, and they are amongst the greatest hospitality dynasties in Ireland, standing alongside the Kellys, the Allens, the Foyles, the Vaughans, the Treacys, the O'Callaghans, the Maguires, the Greens, the O'Haras. The beauty of the house and the grounds, and the stellar quality of the cooking, would have allowed Mark and William to take it easy, but their tenure has seen very radical innovations such as their Rathmullan Good Food Road Food van, a staple of the best Irish festivals, and the imaginative quality and sustainable sourcing of the food they serve in the Weeping Elm restaurant reveals a pair who are always ahead of the curve. Kelan McMichael's tenure in the kitchen has been a match of the ideal chef in the ideal house, for he has a sympathy for and empathy with his ingredients that is precious, and which results in glorious cooking. Make sure to stay for several nights. *Lough Swilly, Rathmullan, County Donegal+ 353 74 9158188 www.rathmullanhouse.com.*

Local Speciality

If you are in the region on a Saturday morning, don't, whatever you do, miss the **Ramelton Country Market.** Legendary for its tray-bakes, breads, vegetarian foods, preserves, home-grown veg and festive goods. Get your elbows ready for the approach, as the cord drops and all the shoppers descend.

Open 11am-12.30pm Sat

Above: Ana's famous American-style cupcakes at The Counter.

Craft Brewery

Kinnegar Craft Brewery of Rathmullan is a hard act to keep up with. One minute, Rick and his team are producing two beers. Then it was three beers. Suddenly it was five, and they fire off special brews in between times, just to stay on their toes, and to celebrate Xmas, or someone's birthday.

The design of the labels and their signature cardboard carrying box is beautiful, and the beer inside is special. The five Kinnegar beers are: Limeburner, a pale ale; Rustbucket, a rye ale; Yannaroddy, their porter; Scraggy Bay, an India pale ale; and Devil's Backbone, an amber ale. They are the wine of the county, and every WAW voyager needs to try all the wines of the counties as you head along the trail, so the Kinnegar beers are the perfect place to start this exuberant exploration.

Rick Le Vert, Rathmullan, County Donegal + 353 74 915 8875 www.kinnegarbrewing.com

2
North West Dunfanaghy to Donegal town

The Green Man

Eileen and Neil draw in lots of interesting foods from near and far in this essential shop, everything from Donegal sea vegetables to Ainé's chocolates to Glastry Farm ice cream to wines from Richard in Letterkenny's The Counter to the brilliant Filligan's Preserves. Essential. *Main Street, Dunfanaghy, County Donegal + 353 74 910 0800. Open daily.*

The Mill Restaurant

Derek Alcorn always credits his kitchen crew at the foot of his menus, a gesture that is typical of his generosity as a chef. He is a self-effacing guy, an old-school chef who stays in his kitchen and cooks great food for the happy residents of this great restaurant with rooms, and for diners. His menus are also beautifully concise and composed – half a dozen starters including a soup; fine mains including a good vegetarian choice. The truth of the matter, however, is that choosing is painful: you want the lot – Irish rabbit bon bons with guinea fowl, parsnip purée, grapes and oat crumble; duck egg with goat's cheese; Cranford scallops with a pea nage and Killult spinach; Ballyare beef with banana shallot and celeriac cannelloni; Killybegs cod with prosciutto mash and a pea and buttermilk velouté; lemon tart with lemon curd macaroons and lime ice cream. Value for money is exceptional, the service from Susan Alcorn and her team is excellent, and the experience of The Mill is simply sublime. The rooms are beautiful and ageless, and the location of the house and the restaurant, beside New Lake on the edge of Dunfanaghy, is an enchantment all by itself. No wonder everyone's a regular. *Figart, Dunfanaghy, County Donegal + 353 74 913 6985 www.themill-restaurant.com*

WILD ATLANTIC WAY

Craft Brewery

Muckish Mountain Brewery
Janet and Leo Harkin's first beer is the nutty Miner's Red Ale, made with centennial hops and dark crystal malt. Hunt it down in good pubs throughout the county. *www.muckishmountain-brewery.com*

The Cove

This restaurant and tapas bar has an unprepossessing exterior, but there is nothing unprepossessing about Siobhan Sweeney's vivid, Asian-accented cooking. There is an Ottolenghi-like exactness about her food, and she loves the zestiness of limes and the heat of chilli. But there is also a Ballymaloe-school rootedness to her work, so it's earthy as well, and the combination makes for great eating. Peter Byrne runs the room with good humour, and there are smashing beers and wines to kick off the evening in the bar upstairs. *Port na Blagh, Dunfanaghy, County Donegal + 353 74 9136300 Open dinner.*

Starfish Café and Bistro

With its laid-back, bricolage design style, and the authentic rusticity of the cooking, Victoria Massey's Starfish Café is just the sort of destination you want to find in a seasidey place like Dunfanaghy. They cook and serve good Donegal beef, fresh local fish and shellfish, turf smoked salmon from Carrigart, and with some good music from local musicians it's very easy to linger longtime. *Main Street, Dunfanaghy, County Donegal + 353 87 32997169 www.starfishcafeandbistro.com. Open daily. Evening Bistro open weekends and in summertime.*

Olde Glen Bar and Restaurant

The Olde Glen has always been a cult destination in County Donegal for great drinks and great cooking, and continues in that exalted vein under Cormac Walsh's direction. The bar is a sure-fire classic, a true original that dates back a couple of hundred years, and which has worn those years well. Make sure to get there early in order to get a table to enjoy some excellent seafood and good, imaginative cooking in the restaurant at the back. And get Aengus to pull you a pint of Rustbucket from Kinnegar Brewery to start the evening in style. *Carrigart, County Donegal + 083 1585777 Restaurant open dinner.*

Danny Minnie's

The O'Donnell family's restaurant with rooms must be one of the longest established restaurants and bars in County Donegal, with a history stretching back over many generations. The dining room is grand and ceremonial, a place for special occasions, a place to enjoy Brian O'Donnell's cooking in classic combinations such as venison with celeriac purée, or Hereford sirloin with pepper, brandy and cream sauce, or medallions of

monkfish with crab bisque sauce. The well-appointed rooms make for luxurious lodging. *Annagry, County Donegal + 353 74 9548201 www.dannyminnies.ie*

Nancy's Bar

How could you not love a traditional Donegal bar that describes its seafood chowder as "very fishy"! How cool is that? Well, cool is what Nancy's Bar is. It's been made famous by the hard work of the McHugh family, who have kept it the way it should be — a warren of cosy rooms — and just made it better with the passing of time, thanks to offering the best cooking they can. *Front Street, Ardara, County Donegal + 353 74 9541187.*

The West End Café

Charlie and Philomena's café is a legendary destination, known principally for their famous fish and chips, freshly cooked and a wonderful demonstration of the fryer's art. But the menu offers much more besides, and the cooking is generous and real. *Main Street, Ardara, County Donegal + 353 74 9541656. Open daily and early evening.*

Local Food

Donegal Rapeseed Oil led the way amongst the wave of modern Irish rapeseed oils, and it has pretty much conquered the country as the go-to cooking oil for both professional and domestic chefs throughout Ireland. It's health-filled DNA make it an essential part of the kitchen armoury, along with a very high smoking point which makes it splendidly versatile.

Oakfield Demesne, Raphoe, County Donegal
+ 353 74 914 5386
donegalrapeseedoilco.com

⸗ Tí Linn

Tí Linn is a coffee shop and craft shop which is part of the Slieve League Cliffs Centre at Carrick. You might wend your way out west to see the Bunglass Cliffs, the highest sea cliffs in Europe, but the good food, excellent coffee and beautiful crafts in Paddy and Siobhan's stylish Tí Linn will give you another reason to return, thanks to Paddy's barista skills and Siobhan's delicious cooking. *Teelin, Carrick, County Donegal + 353 74 973 9077 www.slieveleaguecliffs.ie*

⸗ Castle Murray House

Castle Murray is a restaurant with rooms, and offers some of Donegal's most jaw-dropping views out over St. John's Point. Many people order their classic dishes time after time – the prawns and monkfish in garlic butter gratinated with mozzarella, then the roast Silverhill duck breast with confit red onion purée and port jus, then the warm Belgian chocolate cake with coconut ice cream. All delicious, all good, and whilst you might point out what they are missing – the Inver Bay oysters with chive beurre blanc; the scallops with beetroot croquettes; the halibut and crab with roast butternut squash; the Caribbean trifle – part of the reason for the success of this lovely restaurant with rooms over the last twenty five years is the fact that their classic dishes are, in effect, bomb proof: they deliver them perfectly every time. Good rooms upstairs to rest your head and get ready for the next part of the WAW. *Dunkineely, County Donegal + 353 74 973 7022 www.castlemurray.com.*

⸗ The Village Tavern

Enda O'Rourke's tavern in Mountcharles is one of the guiding lights behind the Donegal Good Food Taverns. The founding philosophy and mission statement of the DGFT is not just practised in The Village Tavern, it is exemplified: Enda sources his fish and shellfish from the ports of Inver and Killybegs; he works hand in glove with Larry Masterson of the nearby Blissberry Farm to grow produce in raised beds and polytunnels, and the result is here to be enjoyed in deft and delicious cooking: summer lobster salad with marinated watermelon; pan-seared scallops with slow-braised tomato broth; seafood taster board; hand-dived scallop gratin; Drimerone lamb with pea risotto; turbot with local crabmeat. Note that you can buy the kitchen's breads and cakes to take away. *Main Street, Mountcharles, County Donegal + 353 74 973 5622 www.villagetavern.ie*

Aroma

In August 2013, Tom and Arturo of the invaluable Aroma, at the Donegal Craft Village, reported that they had just enjoyed 'our busiest August ever!' For a business like Aroma, which is but a tiny single room and which is perennially packed, to show their best ever results really tells you all you need to know about one of the best places to eat in Donegal. What happens with Aroma is simple: people come here for the first time, eat the food, buy the breads, and then they keep coming back, time and again, and the reason why is simply because it is so consistent, so good, so reliable, and the food is so delicious. Arturo cooks European staples – risotto; polenta; pasta – just as well as he cooks his native chimichangas and quesadillas – and Tom's baking is superlative: if you haven't had the Tunisian orange cake, you haven't lived. Aroma has the most dedicated customers, and everyone you meet is a regular. *The Craft Village, Donegal Town, County Donegal + 353 74 972 3222. www.donegalcraftvillage.com/aroma.html Open daily.*

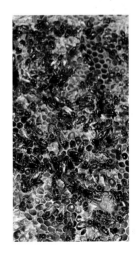

The Blueberry Tearoom

The Blueberry is a small, flower-bedecked room where Brian and Ruperta Gallagher takes care of everyone as if they were family and where tasty, clever food makes sure that everyone who visits comes back. The honesty and hard work of this couple is inspiring, and don't miss Ruperta's great puddings and desserts. *Castle Street, Donegal, County Donegal + 353 74 972 2933. Open daily and early evening.*

Craft Brewery

Don't miss Brendan O'Reilly's celebrated bar and wine shop, **Dicey Reilly's,** in Ballyshannon. It's here they brew **Donegal Blonde,** Mr O'Reilly's fine, crisp beer, and the wine shop is the best in the region.

Market Street, Ballyshannon, County Donegal + 353 71 985 1371 www.donegalbrewingcompany.com

⸸ The Olde Castle Bar & Restaurant

The Olde Castle is the star of Donegal town, for Seoirse and Maeve O'Toole are pushing all the right buttons here in this beautifully restored bar and restaurant. It's a place for both visitors and locals, as visitors can enjoy the good local seafoods that they hope and expect to find in Donegal – Donegal Bay mussels; lobster; Mullaghmore crab; Greencastle haddock – as well as Irish stew and Wicklow venison pie and braised Sligo lamb shank. For locals, the menus offer smart, accessible cooking – triple club sandwich; cheddar cheese beef burger; Maeve's prawn salad. And don't miss their excellent craft beer, Red Hugh Brew. *Tirconnell Street, Donegal, County Donegal + 353 74 972 1262 www.oldecastlebar.com. Open bar lunch and restaurant dinner.*

⸸ The Courthouse

It's just a little jaunt from Bundoran to pretty Kinlough, across the county border into County Leitrim, to find The Courthouse, a lovely restaurant with rooms. 'There was a nice twist on many 'standard' dishes that elevated them to something unique, interesting and memorable', a friend wrote after enjoying dinner in Piero Melis's spirited restaurant. Unique. Interesting. Memorable. We couldn't agree more. Our most recent dinner featured several dishes that were nothing other than outstanding: a Mullaghmore lobster pappardella with light korma and basil sauce; incredible home-made duck ravioli with white ragu; beautiful john dory with mascarpone and crab sauce; sublime veal saltimbocca with mozzarella, Parma ham and a white wine sauce. The food was gracious, subtle and sublime, and so was the service. To make the most of the evening, you can stay in the rooms upstairs, which are simple and affordable, and enjoy the Iselis wines from Mr Melis's native Sardinia. A lovely place, and a great getaway. *Main Street, Kinlough, County Leitrim +353 71 984 2391 www.thecourthouserest. com. Open dinner and Sun lunch.*

Sligo Bay to Erris Head & the Mullet Peninsula

If you are walking the beaches and headlands of Sligo and it should start to rain, don't worry. In fifteen minutes the weather will be transformed from squally showers to beaming sunshine, and instead of being soaking you will be sweating. Sligo is mercurial, always changing, always elusive, much like the mighty waves that draw surfers from all over the world to wave shrines from Mullaghmore to Enniscrone.

WILD ATLANTIC WAY

Eithna's By The Sea

Eithna O'Sullivan is the great food heroine of Sligo, and her seafood restaurant right at the harbour in Mullaghmore has served as a beacon of creative and imaginative cooking for many years. Ms O'Sullivan's seafood cookery pushes all the right buttons, often thanks to the inspired use of foraged seaweeds in dishes such as alaria baked hake, or nori sticky toffee pudding and once you have tried the grilled mackerel with seaweed pesto, or the seaweed and blackberry compote served with some crunchy meringues, you will also want to get a jar or several of Eithna's delicious seaweed condiments to bring home. *The Harbour, Mullaghmore, County Sligo + 353 86 851 5607 www.bythesea.ie*

Seacrest Guest House

Eithna O'Sullivan also runs this comfortable guesthouse in Mullaghmore, which is only 50 metres from a Blue Flag beach. There are three rooms for guests, all fully appointed. Surfers should note that Mullaghmore is one of the top ten big wave surf spots in the world, so get the board out. *Mullaghmore, County Sligo + 353 71 9266468 www.seacrestguesthouse. com*

Lang's of Grange

Lang's is as authentic a bar as any traveller could hope to find, and the Burke family offer good pub grub – steak sandwich; fish and chips; bangers and mash – perfect for enjoying with a pint of Donegal Blonde. *Grange, County Sligo + 353 71 916 3105 www.langs.ie. Open lunch and dinner.*

Drumcliffe Tea House

The Tea House is where you go for tea and buns and some retail therapy when you pay your respects to W.B. Yeats in Drumcliffe graveyard. *Drumcliffe, County Sligo + 353 71 914 4956 www. drumcliffeteahouse.ie Open day time.*

Vintage Lane

All the design elements are artfully mismatched in this quirky and cute café, but the cooking and baking are straight ahead delicious, whether it's a savoury goat's cheese tart or a sweet lemon drizzle cake. There is an excellent craft and food market also held here on Saturday mornings, so that is the optimum time to pay a visit. But anytime the wind is whistling over Ben Bulben you will find a warm fire blazing in Vintage Lane and an excellent cup of coffee, served with charm and good cheer by a team who enjoy their work and who are forging a fine reputation. *Branleys Yard, Rathcormac, County Sligo + 353 87 662 2600. Open daily.*

Markets

Sligo has developed a cracking market, so look out for Irish organic meats, Bluebell Farm organic nettle pesto; J&M's veggie treats; eggs from Ballysadare; Trevor's cheeses; Organic Centre plants; Kinneden organic vegetables; Shanvaus honeys; Gerry's fish, and lots more. Just smashing.

Sligo IT Sports Field Car Park, Saturday morning.

The Beltra Country Market also runs on Saturday morning and has a coffee room as well as selling local produce, home baking and local crafts.

Harry's Bar & Gastro Pub

Five generations of the Ewing family have welcomed visitors to Rosses Point, and this nautically-themed bar offers good cooking, so turn up for baked Atlantic cod, venison pie, spit-roasted lamb, all made from scratch and served by a dedicated team.
Rosses Point, Sligo, County Sligo + 353 71 917 7173 www.harryrossespoint.com

Coach Lane

Orla and Andy serve food both in the upstairs restaurant and in the bar at Donaghy's, but it's the steak frites served upstairs that brings many people back to Coach lane. Ingredients are carefully sourced, and there are good seafood choices as well as those fine rib-eyes and sirloins. *1 Lord Edward Street, Sligo, County Sligo + 353 71 916 2417 www.coachlane.ie*

Eala Bhan Restaurant

Anthony Gray runs both Eala Bhan restaurant in Sligo town and its sister restaurant, Tra Bhan, out in Strandhill, where the resturant is upstairs from the much-loved The Strand Bar. The cooking in Eala Bhan is ambitious and imaginative – 8-hour Sligo pork belly with chorizo jelly; pan-seared scallops with kataifi prawns and crab bon bon; duo of Sligo lamb with lamb pie and lamb rack; blackberry bakewell tart – and there is a smart, city-like room in which to enjoy chef Seamus Thompson's modern riffs on classic dishes. Out in Strandhill at Tra Bhan the cooking is simpler – spicy chicken wings; fillet steak with garlic butter; supreme of chicken with pesto mash – and then head downstairs for some great music. *Sligo town, County Sligo + 353 71 9145823 www.ealabhan.ie. Open lunch and dinner.*

Fabio's

Fabio's is a tiny kiosk-like shop selling home-made ice-cream, which is made fresh on site with local ingredients and fresh fruit. *2a Wine Street, Sligo, County Sligo + 353 87 177 2732 Open daily.*

The Glasshouse

The excellent central location of The Glasshouse, and the good views over The Garavogue river makes it the best choice for staying in Sligo. The staff are enthusiastic, the decor has a funky, retro vibe with lots of boldly coloured and stylised artworks and lots of lime and orange on the colour palette. *Swan Point, Sligo, County Sligo + 353 71 914 9170 www.theglasshouse. ie*

Gourmet Parlour

'We don't compromise', Catherine Farrell will tell you as a way to explain the success and the longevity of the Gourmet Parlour, one of the most distinguished food destinations in Sligo.

Opposite: Lyon's Café

'Everything is homemade - if we make a ham sandwich the ham is boiled in house, the mayo is home-made with free-range eggs'. When Aoife Cox of the *McKennas' Guides* paid a visit, the Gourmet Parlour rendered her helpless: 'Within seconds - seconds, I tell you - I succumbed to the charms of apple tart, homemade blackcurrant jam and a spinach and mushroom pie. The lure of authentic and honest baking was simply irresistible'. It has been that way ever since the girls first featured in our books back in 1991: authentic and honest, and ever-reliable. *Bridge Street, Sligo, County Sligo + 353 71 914 4617 www.gourmetparlour.com*

Seaweed Baths

Kilcullen's Hot Water Seaweed Baths
is 100 years old. A century of service, a century spent harnessing the goodness of seaweeds and sea water for the benefit of our collective health. There are other seaweed baths, but there are no seaweed baths like Kilcullen's, with its traditional steam boxes, its traditional big baths, its fresh, tangy, kelpy, sea salty seaweeds. A visit here is one of life's great pleasures.

Enniscrone, County Sligo + 353 9636238 www.kilcullenseaweedbaths.com

Hargadon's
Joe Grogan and Miriam Harte and their team run a superbly managed organisation in the legendary Hargadon's Bar, one of Ireland's best-known pubs. Their reputation today is founded on cracking food and superb value. But the dishes aren't inexpensive because of low-quality ingredients: in fact, their sourcing is superb – Silverhill duck; Burren smoked salmon; Clarke's meats; Charlie Kelly's shellfish. Great wines from their own wine shop complete a happy picture. *4 O'Connell Street, Sligo, County Sligo + 353 71 915 3709 www.hargadons.com*

Kate's Kitchen
'The impossibly well-stocked Kate's Kitchen', is how Aoife Cox describes Kate, Beth and Jane's magnificent emporium. 'All the classic artisan brands are here,' says Aoife, 'Sheridan's, Ummera, Gubbeen, Janet's Country Fayre, they were all there, along with Natasha's kale crunchies, and far cheaper than you'll get them in Dublin. It is exactly the kind of place where you would expect to find the most up-to-the-minute artisan brands'. *3 Castle Street, Sligo, County Sligo + 353 71 914 3022 www.kateskitchensligo.ie*

Lyon's Café
Gary Stafford knows food. He understands what good cooking requires, he minds his dishes and mentors them to be as good as they can be. And the result for the devoted customers in Lyon's Café is delicious, authentic food, food with trueness and goodness, food that zings with health and energy. Lyon's Café has a bright, cheery atmosphere, the sound of happy customers enjoying today's vegetable tagine, or a steak and cheese sandwich, or a proper burger with couscous. 'Everything made for taste' we noted one day: Lyon's Café – Made For Taste. The staff, of course, are top notch. *Lyon's Department Store, Quay Street, Sligo, County Sligo + 353 71 914 2969 www.garystafford.com. Open day time.*

Osta

Brid Torrades is one of Sligo's greatest food heroes, putting delicious local foods to use every day in the most imaginative and creative way, all the way from breakfast to their super tapas menus. *Unit 2, Weir View House, Stephen Street, Sligo, County Sligo + 353 71 914 4639 www.osta.ie. Open daytime and early evening.*

Shell's Café and Little Shop

Shell's is so good that it merits a trip to Strandhill, all by itself. Jane and Myles are smart, hip and experienced, and together they bring all the best elements of their travels and their cultural accumulations to play in their café. So, head to Strandhill for Persian couscous with grilled chicken, for rainbow trout with barley risotto, for herby fishcakes with mayo and fries, for slow-cooked beef brisket with gravy. Get up early for their splendid breakfasts, and pray for sunshine so you can eat them on the deck. They have a sweet little shop, they have supper club evenings, and they have finally got around to writing that book. Everyone's favourite. *Strandhill, County Sligo + 353 71 912 2938 www.shellscafe.com Open day time.*

The Strand Bar

The Strand is where the locals drink, it's where the surfers drink, it's where folk from Sligo come to for

a drink and a bite to eat. The owners are surfing champions themselves, but you don't need to own a board to enjoy The Strand. There is excellent music, and the place is perennially packed to the rafters, as it has been for 100 years. *Strandhill, Sligo, County Sligo + 353 71 916 8140 www.thestrandbar.ie. Open lunch and dinner.*

Strandhill Lodge & Suites

This small boutique hotel is the best choice in Strandhill, and manager David McCoy and his team look after their guests well and maintain their twenty two rooms to an excellent standard. The rooms are very comfortable and sleekly designed. *Strandhill, County Sligo + 353 71 912 2122 www.strandhilllodgeandsuites.com*

The Beach Bar

The Beach Bar is well named, for the sand from the beach actually blows right up into the car park outside the McDermott family's pub.

It's a classic, low-ceilinged, thatched cottage and was a very well-kept secret before the surfers discovered Aughris Head – when we first came here almost thirty years ago you practically had the place to yourself, save for a few locals.

That isn't the case any more, for tasty food and perfect pints and loads of surf schools bring in the crowds during the summer, and everyone wants a piece of this uniquely characterful bar and, after the waves have hammered you, everyone is hungry for pan-fried hake with pesto and scallops with stir-fried vegetables and mussels with garlic bread. *Aughris, County Sligo + 353 71 9176465 www.thebeachbarsligo.com*

Below: The Beach Bar, Aughris

The Pilot Bar

The Pilot is a really popular pub both for drinks and for their cooking, so once you are off the surf board or out of the seaweed baths, head here for refreshment. *Main Street, Inniscrone, County Sligo + 353 96 36161 www.thepilotbar.ie. Open lunch and dinner.*

Clarke's Seafood Delicatessen

The Clarke brothers run benchmark shops in both Ballina and Westport. For decades the family have been famous for their smoked salmon, but in fact that expertise runs through every aspect of a model modern fish business, so their prepared fish dishes and their deli fish concoctions are just as fine as their wet fish and their smoked fish. You simply won't find a more customer-focused business than Clarke's, which makes shopping in the Mayo store a particular treat, everytime. *O'Rahilly Street, Ballina, County Mayo + 353 96 21022 www.clarkes.ie*

Heffernan's Fine Foods and the Heifer & Hen Café

Heffernan's seems to be a business blessed with eternal youth. It's actually more than 50 years old – established in 1961 by John Heffernan – and yet it is as hip-to-the-trip as anywhere in the West. Like so many other Mayo destinations, Heffernan's reinvented itself a few years back, adding a spiffing deli and café whilst continuing the butchery business, which is founded on Mayo meats, coming direct from their own abattoir, where Anthony Heffernan oversees everything. There is care evident at every juncture here, from Bridie's brown bread to your supper striploin, and upstairs now they have the Heifer & Hen Café, so head here for crab cakes with Asian slaw, and baked cod with sautéed sea vegetables and silver hake with pont neuf chips and peperonata. Heffernen's is pretty much a one-stop shop for whatever you need and want. *4 Market Square, Ballina, County Mayo + 353 96 21218 www.heffernansfinefoods.com. Open lunch and dinner.*

Market Kitchen

'I can tell you very quickly and simply that I had one of the best meals of the year so far up in Market Kitchen in Ballina last week', writes our man out West. 'The food really was stunning, particularly considering the price. It seems to be very much a team-based effort in the kitchen, but what a team: they really have a great system going there.' Susan and Kieran certainly have the good system going here, upstairs at Murphy Bros' famous pub, and the cooking is rockin': mushrooms à la crème; organic salmon with a leek, prawn and cheese pie; chump of lamb with polenta fried feta; Elphin pork belly with black pudding potatoes; chocolate ganache pudding with pistachio ice cream. Great value for money, excellent food for the children, nice food downstairs in the bar, and there is terrific energy in the Market Kitchen. *Clare Street, Ballina, County Mayo + 353 96 78538 www.marketkitchen.ie. Open dinner and Sun lunch.*

Mary's Cottage Kitchen

Mary's of Ballycastle is such a sweet, old-style bakery and café, unpretentious, welcoming, and blessed with good cooking and good baking that is agelessly enjoyable. *Main Street, Ballycastle, County Mayo + 353 96 43361*

Polke's

Polke's is a darling wee public house, with a wee shop at the front, and that wee dram on the counter in the bar at the back has your name on it. And do check out all the wonderful art works gifted by visiting artists. *Main Street, Ballycastle, County Mayo + 353 96 43016.*

Stella Maris

Frances and Terence's stellar Stella Maris country house and restaurant has been one of the catalysts, and one of the leading lights, of County Mayo's culinary renaissance, one of the key players in the county's invention of itself as one of the best places to visit in Ireland to find creative, imaginative and daring cooking.

When we first wrote about Mr McSweeney and Ms Kelly's country house, way back in 2003 just after they opened, we predicted it would be one of the stars of the following ten years. Everything that a great country house needed was in situ, most of all the dynamism of this talented couple and the character of their beautiful, seaside house.

Today, Stella Maris is recognised as one of the best places to eat and stay in County Mayo and in Ireland, and it has gained that reputation thanks to the devotion and discipline of this couple. Ms Kelly's cooking, in particular, is all her own, modestly and precisely executed in every detail. We have described her cooking as "Proustian", for you can eat dishes here that torment your memory with delight for years afterwards. It is cooking that comforts while it delights, a very feminine country cooking that has the most complete confidence of all: the confidence to be simple. *Ballycastle, County Mayo + 353 96 43322 www.stellamarisireland.com*

Léim Siar

Hannah Quigley's fine B&B is way, way, way out west at Blacksod, way, way, way down the peninsula, far, far, far from the madding crowds. So you are here for the beaches and the sunsets, the stars and the skies, but also for Hannah's scones and her boxty with home-grown tomatoes, for the local sausages and the garden vegetables, for the fruits from the garden. Do note that there is also self-catering accommodation available. *Blacksod, Belmullet, County Mayo + 353 97 85004 www.leimsiar.com*

4
Achill to Westport

The great journalist and writer John Healy was a Mayo man, born in Charlestown, and in his classic book *No One Shouted Stop* he recalls market day in the town: 'Today at the back of your mind you can still smell Wednesday... the new hay, the brown smell of the creaking egg baskets... of fresh meat... fresh herrings and dilisk, salty tanged in this inland town... the camphored black frieze of the widow woman's best coat... the smell of the horses and donkeys... of the packing from the tea chests of the travelling man with the delph and the hardware: 'everything for the home and the farm' was the chirp of the dealer who may have had a home somewhere but never saw a farm... the day and the town was a symphony of sound and smell.'

The symphony of sound and smell is back in County Mayo these days, but it is re-born, and it is vigorous and dynamic, found in cafés and shops, found in hotels and restaurants. In the last ten years, one of the best food cultures of the West Coast has been fashioned here, and it's a food culture that has really found its mojo, founded on local foods, cooked by local chefs. There is a real sense of pride about the county's food and the late John Healy – a serious food lover – would have been delighted to see the energy there is in his native county today.

WILD
ATLANTIC
WAY

Opposite: An Port Mor

Local Food

Cuinneog butter is a hand-made butter made from County Mayo milk, produced from a little garden unit just outside Castlebar. The Butler family have been producing this precious product for twenty five years and today it's quite widely distributed, so you often see its distinctive orange label in supermarkets. Cuinneog is also turning up on more and more restaurant menus, with the best Irish restaurants highlighting that they use this very special ingredient. They also make a very special buttermilk, which is a great treat to drink, thanks to its thirst-slaking qualities, and of course it is essential for making the most perfect loaf of Irish soda bread. The word cuinneog is Irish for churn.

Above and opposite:
Mulranny Park

Mulranny Park

Ollie O'Regan is turning out some of the prettiest plates of food imaginable in The Nephin Restaurant: you feast first with your eyes, then get to work. This isn't food: this is art. This is painting with ingredients. It's so gorgeous. And it's the kind of thing that Mr O'Regan, chef in the Nephin Restaurant, achieves with every plate – you never ate so well with your eyes as you do at the Nephin. Mr O'Regan has simplified his food, and it has made his cooking better because everything on the plate is there because it has to be there – the smoked celeriac purée with Angus beef; the horseradish with feather blade terrine; the black pudding and sage polenta with Sean Kelly's lamb; the broad bean hollandaise with monkfish.

The room is as beautiful as the food, and value is exceptional. Elsewhere, the hotel is packed with walkers and cyclists marching through the Greenway, and manager Dermot Madigan and his team demonstrate at every juncture that they are masters of their art.

The Mulranny is one of the jewels of the West Coast, a jewel for the Greenway, a jewel for the Wild Atlantic Way, a place of true Mayo enchantment. *Mulranny, County Mayo + 353 98 36000 www. mulrannyparkhotel.ie. Open for bar lunch with restaurant opening for dinner.*

Achill Cliff House Hotel

Teresa McNamara's little hotel is a sweet, welcoming place and Ms McNamara works hard at her cooking. The menus read rather straight ahead – garlic mushrooms; deep-fried brie; duck with ginger and orange sauce – but the cooking is lively and flavourful, and extremely enjoyable, especially if you have built up an appetite from a day on the surf or hiking the cliffs. The location is brilliant if you want to golf, cycle and surf, and the McNamaras offer true hospitality, and some amazing views of Keel beach and the Minaun cliffs. *Keel, Achill Island, County Mayo + 353 98 43400 www.achillcliff.com*

Local Food

There are a variety of unique styles of lamb to be enjoyed on the WAW, but one of the most distinctive and special is the lamb which is born, pastured and cooked on Achill Island itself. See the entry for the Calvey family of Achill, who have half a century of experience in breeding and preparing the **Mayo Blackface Mountain Lamb.**

Bervie

The sea comes close to the house at Bervie: all you have to do is walk down the garden, open the gate, and there you are on the beach. Whatever your age, it is a primal experience. The cooking chimes with the location perfectly in this B&B – smoked Achill salmon with pickled vegetables, then the magnificent Achill lamb with pea purée (no other lamb tastes like Achill lamb), and then bread and butter pudding. Bervie is as close as the Wild Atlantic Way actually gets to the wild Atlantic, and if you are a surfing dude, or a painting dude, then there is no better place than Bervie to evoke the magic of Achill. *Keel, Achill Island, County Mayo + 353 98 43114 www.bervieachill.com*

Blackfield

Surf school. Café. Fashion atelier. And double-decker bus. Gerry Brannigan's Blackfield really has the lot, and this sort of left-field adventure is just what you dream of finding when you cross over to the island from the mainland with your board on the roof. Lovely coffees will bring you back to life after the waves have smashed your body and your resolve. Blackfield is a member of the great Greenway Adventures group. *Closhreid, Achill Island, County Mayo + 353 98 43590 www.blackfield.com. Open daily.*

The Gourmet Greenway

Farmhouse cheeses. Organic farm eggs. Mayo mezze plates. Curraun blue trout. Kelly's Gourmet Greenway black pudding. Murrevagh honey. Cutting-edge west coast cookery. Dana's banana butter. Marlene's chocolates. All these, and more, are the signature foods of one of the most inspired innovations in Irish artisan foods, County Mayo's **Gourmet Greenway.** Some of the producers in the GG are in, on and around the Wild Atlantic Way, and you will find their foods in shops and markets on the route. For others you would need to make a small detour – into Castlebar, for instance – to sample their delights. The Gourmet Greenway grew out of the cycling track known as the Great Western Greenway, and has since given birth to the Greenway Adventures, a bunch of outdoorsy wildguys who will teach you how to kitesurf, abseil, kayak, ride a pony, catch a sea fish, ride a mountain bike or just explore the county on foot. So, work up an appetite on a windsurf board, then sate that appetite by discovering Mayo's best foods cooked by Mayo's best cooks. It's a mighty mix of the best the county has to offer, and no visitor should miss these inspiring adventures.

Calvey's Restaurant & Wild Mint Deli

The Calvey family rear, process and cook the unique Achill lamb, controlling every part of the operation from farm to fork. And they have been doing it on the island for over fifty years, now, so when you sit down in the restaurant, what you want is six-hour braised organic Achill lamb shank, served with mash. And grilled organic Achill lamb with rosemary potatoes and wild mint jelly. Yes we know there are other things to eat in Maeve Calvey's restaurant, but to be able to eat organic Achill lamb from the producers on Achill Island itself is one of the great experiences of the WAW. Grainne's brand-new Wild Mint Deli is a vital stop for tasty foods to take away. *Keel East, Achill Island, County Mayo + 353 98 43158 www.calveysofachill.com. Open lunch and dinner.*

The Chalet & Keem Bay Fish Products

Gerry Hassett has thirty years' experience as a fish smoker, focusing on organic salmon, mackerel and kippers. With his wife, Julie, Gerry also operates The Chalet which, like the Calvey family's Achill lamb business, has half-a-century of service to Achill. Unmissable destinations and unmissable tastes when visiting on the WAW. *Keel, Achill Island, County Mayo + 353 98 43157. Open dinner.*

Pure Magic at The Lodge

The Pure Magic pizzas got a big shout out when *The Irish Times* asked its readers to find the best pizzas in Ireland. But in addition to their highly-regarded pizzas there is also a restaurant and a bar and a coffee shop and some nice rooms at this activity centre. Their core activities are windsurfing and SUP (Stand-Up Paddle-boarding) but they can also organise bikes, horses, you name it, all the better to build up that mega appetite for a mega-dinner, and the the sleep of the just for those who have spent the day on the waves. *Slievemore Road, Dugort, Achill, County Mayo + 353 98 43859 www.puremagic.ie*

The Kelly Kettle

Many people are surprised to hear that the legendary Kelly Kettle is actually made in Ireland, yet it has been made in Ireland by four generations of the Kelly family. 'Camping equipment for wilderness survival, emergency preparedness or disaster kits' it says on the website – and we have to add from personal experience it is absolutely essential for a family picnic day out on the beach. Once you fire it up, you will find everyone on the beach comes over to see this miraculous cauldron in action.

www.kellykettle.com

Craft Brewery

Mescan

is named for Saint Patrick's best friend, who also happened to be his personal brewer. Was Saint Patrick smart, or what? Bart and Cillian brew Belgian-style brews – Bart hails from there – and both share the profession of veterinarian. Setting up their own Mayo microbrewery on the slopes of Croagh Patrick is just the sort of thing a couple of vets might decide to do, so look out for the Mescan Blond, the Belgian-style Porter and the Red Tripel.

⌘ The Blue Bicycle

Tuck into a bowl of carrageen and vegetable soup, in Philly Chamber's cute, cosy The Blue Bicycle, and the world is suddenly in order. The kids are loving their Achill Island BBQ salmon and slices of Carrowholly cheese and hot slices of Sean Kelly's black pudding. Everyone is happy, and you haven't even had a slice of Princess Grace orange cake with orange and cardamom syrup and fresh cream, with hot chocolates for the little ones and a perfect cappuccino for yourself. The sun is shining. The Greenway beckons.
Main Street, Newport, County Mayo + 353 98 41145
www.bluebicycletearooms.com Open daily.

⌘ Kelly's Butchers & Kelly's Kitchen

Sean Kelly is one of the most famous food personalities in Ireland, and he has been one of the most tireless champions on behalf of County Mayo and its food culture. He inspires people in two ways – firstly, by virtue of the superb quality of his meat products and his prize-winning charcuterie creations (this is a man who can make a wedding cake out of black pudding). Secondly, he inspires by example, for he is hard-working and enthusiastic and up-for-it, improving the quality of life for everyone who gets to sample the superlative produce of Kelly's butchers. And get the good taste of Mayo in Kelly's Kitchen, where Shauna Kelly cooks these iconic sausages and puddings, alongside a host of delicious daily specials and a wow! strawberry and fresh cream gateau.
Main Street, Newport, County Mayo + 353 98 41149
www.kellysbutchers.com

Newport House

Newport is one of the great Irish country houses. It is grand, serene, majestic, aristocratic, with cooking that matches all of these attributes, classic cuisine that is led by magnificent local ingredients served in a large, gracious room. Despite its grandeur, it has few airs, but many graces, and staying and eating here is a very special experience. The bar, incidentally, is one of our favourite places in which to have an aperitif. *Newport, County Mayo + 353 98 41222 www.newporthouse.ie*

Below: An Port Mor

An Port Mor

In An Port Mor, chef Frankie Mallon cooks the way he is: it's his own character that comes through in the cooking. He doesn't do styles or fads or the latest thing: he cooks for himself, and of himself. What he likes to do is to arrange beautifully curated foods on a plate, as if he is making a mosaic. He likes sweet, unctuous tastes – pork cheeks; lobster; a crab crust on cod; sweet Mayo lamb – and this signature style makes his food friendly to eat, easy to enjoy. It isn't at all concerned with fashion, he plates up creamy vegetable gratins, beside herbs and flowers and light infused dressings.

The restaurant is a series of narrow rooms presided over by genial, caring staff and with a genial, caring boss in the kitchen. The staff give off a concern that suggests that they don't simply work here: working here is part of who they are, not part of what they do. It doesn't feel like a restaurant : it feels like someone's home. And Mr Mallon doesn't cook like the standard-issue chef: he's special. *Bridge Street, Westport, County Mayo + 353 98 26730 www.an-portmor.com. Open dinner.*

Clew Bay Hotel

Maria and Darren's family-run hotel has a family-run style, which we rather like. The family has a long history of offering hospitality in the town, and they offer good cooking both in Madden's Bar – Clew Bay chowder; loaded potato skins; traditional fish and chips – and in the Riverside Restaurant where the cooking is more formal. Good housekeeping, good service and good value make the Clew Bay a good place to rest your head. *James Street, Westport, County Mayo + 353 98 28088 www.clewbayhotel.com*

Knockranny House Hotel

'Knockranny House not only serves splendid food alongside a very considered wine list but they perform the even more difficult trick of making a relatively modern five-star hotel into something akin to an old school country house hotel - and it's all down to the wonderful people working there.' That is Joe McNamee's summation of the many charms of Knockranny House, one of the jewels of the West Coast, and one of the key players in County Mayo's rise as a serious destination for food lovers. Yes the cooking from Seamus Commons is wonderful – amongst the very best – and yes the wine list is magic. But Knockranny is really a people place, an hotel made special by the distinctive, generous and abiding welcome that the staff exude every minute of the day. That welcome pulls together all the elements of the hotel, making you feel pampered and special. If you can, then try to get here to experience some of their special dinners – Leslie Williams described an autumn game dinner as being 'as good as any I've tasted' – when everything comes together to make simple magic. *Westport, County Mayo + 353 98 28600 www.khh.ie.*

Above: An Port Mor

Market 57

Alongside lots of good kitchen gear and pretty household goods, Market 57 has a splendid selection of local foods and other artisan treats, so it's a good place to bring your shopping list of County Mayo specialities. *67 Bridge Street, Westport, County Mayo + 353 98 27317 www.kitchencookware.ie.*

Marlene's Chocolate Haven

If Marlene's shop is a Chocolate Haven, then that must make Marlene a Chocolate Maven. So, visit the Maven in the Haven for the legendary hot chocolate, great mochas, delicious scones, and loads of chocolate treats. *Limecourt, James Street, Westport, County Mayo + 353 98 24564 www.chocolatehaven.net. Open daily.*

Kate McCormack & Sons

Kate McCormack's is a legendary butcher's shop in Westport, with a history stretching back over six generations, and a stellar reputation amongst local food lovers and local chefs. It's an archetypal shop, white-tiled, with butcher's hooks and just the right feeling and ambience. But it's not just a butcher's, for beside the shop you will find McCormack's coffee shop, which is a lovely space in which to take tea and cakes, and nice simple lunches, whilst you enjoy the paintings in the gallery. *Bridge Street, Westport, County Mayo + 353 98 25619 www.katemccormackandsons.ie. Open daily.*

Matt Molloy's

Matt Molloy is a famous musician – flute player with The Chieftains, don't you know – but in Westport he is famous as a man who runs one of the nicest traditional pubs in Ireland. Molloy's is a classic of the genre – crowded, sociable, affable, with fabulous music every evening, and it's a great place to hunt down the craft beers of Mayo county in the company of all your best mates. *Bridge Street, Westport, County Mayo + 353 98 26655 www.mattmolloy.com*

Craft Brewery

Iain and Caroline Price were the first craft brewery to be established in County Mayo for two centuries, brewing at the **West Mayo Brewery** in their home, Hill Top Farm, in Islandeady. Look out for Clew Bay Sunset, Paddy's Pilgrim Porter and Clifford's Connacht Champion. We love the fact that the brewery is based on a small, working farm.

www.westmayobrewery.com

Local speciality

Andrew Pelham-Byrne's splendid **Carrowholly cheeses** are made with local, raw milk from small farms. As well as the plain version, Andrew flavours others with nettle, cumin, pepper, and garlic and chive. Look out in particular for Old Russet, aged for up to 9 Months: get this at the Westport Market on Thursdays from Andrew's stall.

www.carrowhollycheese.ie

Opposite: Cuinneog Butter
Below: Purple Root Cafe

Pantry and Corkscrew

Dermott and Janice have enjoyed great success in their charming, funky restaurant, The Pantry & Corkscrew, at Westport's Octagon over the last few years. Cooking for dinner service only allows them more time for prep, more time to polish the very winning style of Mr O'Rourke's cooking. He begins with terrific ingredients and then brings a very personal style to the food: the menu, one suspects, are the things Dermott and Janice love to cook and love to eat. Don't miss the courgette and feta fritters, their classic cheddar-and-sage burger, the Dublin Bay prawn and courgette gnocchi, and don't miss the Bocelli estate wines, as you will only find them here. *The Octagon, Westport, County Mayo + 353 98-26977. Open dinner.*

Purple Root Café

Fionnuala McKenna's raw food and vegan café is where you go to get good, pure food that enlivens and detoxes you. Ms McKenna is a great crusader for good food, and a teacher of raw food practices, so come here for that hit of wheatgrass. *James Street, Westport, County Mayo + 353 86 896 7828 Open daily*

Sol Rio

'I set out to find them, wondering if they could really be that good. And they were.' That's Marie-Claire Digby of *The Irish Times* writing about her quest to find, and her discovery of, Jose Barroso's pasteis de nata, the egg-custard pastries Jose makes for the deli in Sol Rio, the hugely popular restaurant that the couple run on Bridge Street. Jose has a sure touch with the pasteis, and with everything else on the menu, in both the ground floor café and the first-floor restaurant. He sources carefully, so everything is imbued with taste and integrity, from the pastas and pizzas to the farmer's style chicken, and there is a lovely menu for children. *Bridge Street, Westport, County Mayo + 353 98 28944 www.solrio.ie. Open breakfast, lunch and dinner.*

Above: Sol Rio

Opposite: Pantry and Corkscrew

Westport Plaza Hotel

Joe and Anne Corcoran's hotel is one of those destinations where things are done correctly. The greeting, the service, the cooking, the housekeeping all sync beautifully here, and the professionalism gladdens the heart. The Corcorans have a very clear vision of creating and keeping a happy workforce as the means by which you create happy guests in an hotel, and they have made this simple, sympathetic philosophy work, both in the Plaza itself and in its larger, adjacent sister hotel, the Castlecourt Hotel. There is an evident sense of commitment from the staff here – nothing is too much trouble, anything you need to know they know already, or will find out for you. This is just the spirit you want to discover when staying in a resort hotel in a holiday town like pretty Westport. *Castlebar Street, Westport, County Mayo + 353 98 51166 www.westportplazahotel.ie.*

Quay Cottage

Kirstin McDonagh has happily re-opened Westport's iconic Quay Cottage, a fact that will delight food lovers who recall the Cottage with much fondness from its days as a trailblazer in Westport's culinary scene. Michel Nagy runs the kitchen, Pascale Soual runs the front of house, and the characterful room and the characterful cooking are right on song: seafood taster plate; confit duck tartlette; monkfish wrapped in smoked pork belly; cod with langoustine bisque; ribeye with confit shallots; Kelly's pork platter; orange and whiskey steamed pudding. The room is charming, and it's always good times in Quay Cottage.

The Quay, Westport, County Mayo + 353 98 50692 www.quaycottage.com. Open lunch and dinner.

Westport Markets

Westport was voted the Best Place to live in Ireland by readers of The Irish Times in 2013. It could also have been voted, Best Place to Have a Food Market, as the town boasts two vigorous markets each week. The country market takes place in the town hall on Thursday mornings, whilst the food and craft market lines up on the Mall beside the river, from early on Saturday morning. See you there.

Sage Westport

Sometimes, mixed metaphors are just what you need. A friend, after a meal at Sage in Westport, wrote that chef-proprietor Shteryo Yurukov 'really seems to have found his feet/spread his wings'. Yeah, you know what he means. Mr Yurukov has been working in Westport and other points in Mayo over the last dozen years, but Sage is the first time he gets his name over the door, along with his partner, Eva Ivanova, who manages the room. Together, they are fashioning something rather special, and have created a destination address in Westport. The chef, in finding his feet, has been given the chance to spread his wings. Everything is sure-footed: lobster and scallop gratin with an incredible coastline salad and samphire fritters; calamari with anchovy mayonnaise; a gorgeous salad of Mayo leaves and flowers from Joe Kelly; Friendly Farmer chicken with pancetta and mozzarella stuffing; amazing crab ravioli with chanterelle mushroom sauce. *10 High Street, Westport, County Mayo + 353 098 56700. Open dinner.*

Shopping List

Westport is a great place to stock up on local specialities, so in the market and in the shops look out for: Kelly's puddings and sausages; Jack & Eddie's bacon and sausages; Carrowholly cheese; Murrevagh honey; A Taste of Days Gone By jams and preserves; Marlene's chocolates; Achill Sea Salt; Harvest Moon hummous and pestos; Red's Sauces; Cherry Blossom Bakery breads; Keem Bay smoked fish; Cuinneog country butter; Bean West Coffee; Wildwood vinegars.

The Tavern

For more than a dozen years now, Myles and Ruth have been making people happy in Murrisk, sourcing local foods, cooking them wisely and well, and offering excellent drinks and superb service, in both the bar and the restaurant at The Tavern. Mr O'Brien's cooking is not just honest and generous: it is also wise and logical, so in addition to the restaurant there is splendid seafood in the bar, a great children's menu, and it's the place for Achill sea trout, or wild Clew Bay lobster with sea lettuce and mixed leaf salad. Terrific. *Murrisk, Westport, County Mayo + 353 98 64060*

5
Inishbofin &
Connemara

The moon-struck plateaux of Connemara can play tricks on the eye of the traveller, throwing mirages into focus as you pitch, toss and turn on the roads that wind around the calm lakes, the sodden bogs and the rock-freckled fields. Those clouds rising out of the gap between the mountains look like smoke from a forest fire: this road seems as if it is destined to pitch you right into that lake that lies ahead: those hills appear to be many miles away but then, suddenly, you are upon them, as if the intervening land had vanished beneath you.

There is no official boundary to Connemara, no final lines which call it to a halt or announce its arrival. Distances become mere speculations of the mind, and in amongst the hills there is a feeling that the separate culture of this part of the west includes its own perspective.

WILD
ATLANTIC
WAY

♪ The Beach, Days Bar and B&B

Orla Day and Adrian Herlihy run this idyllic bar and B&B on Inishbofin island. They are serious about food and serious about beer, and their fantastic location and resources mean you can quite happily expect lobster on the menu, with a glass of 8 Degrees Amber Ella or a bottle of McGrath's Black to pair with it or some Stonewell cider with supreme of chicken and Moran's of Clifden black pudding, and they do a good sweet potato gnocchi to match the sweetness of monkfish brochettes. There are cosy rooms in the B&B, nicely appointed and colourful, and don't be thinking about how hard it is going to be when it's actually time to leave. *The Beach, Days Bar, Inishbofin, County Galway + 353 95 45829. Open lunch and dinner.*

Local Food

The **Cleggan Seaweed Co** has always had a vision of their seaweeds as a connoisseur product, something that sits comfortably in gourmet hampers, or on the shelves of the best delicatessens. Their Sea Pickle looks like the sort of jar you would expect to buy in Fortnum & Mason. They have always demonstrated confidence and finesse with their boxes of seaweed – five varieties, which are hand-picked from the clean local shoreline and packed and sold without need of any further processing.

www.clegganseaweed.com

Delphi Lodge

The reason Peter Mantle's country house and estate is world-renowned is not just because of what it is, but also because of what it is not. Yes, it is an especially beautiful house in one of the most beautiful places in Ireland – if not the world. But equally important is the fact that Delphi doesn't try to be an hotel, or to ape hotel-style service. It has stubbornly set its face against the modern blandness many people think of as luxury. So, instead it is quaint, a place that is comfortable with itself, which means you will be comfortable with it too. In Delphi, they know what they can do best, and their best is what they do. It's a simple thing, but it demands a quiet confidence. *Leenane, County Galway + 353 95 42222 www.delphilodge.ie.*

Renvyle House Hotel

Ronnie and Tim, manager and chef of Renvyle House, are one of the great double acts in Irish hospitality and food. Between them, Mr Ronnie Counihan and Mr Tim O'Sullivan have created a manifesto for Renvyle that is one of the most compelling examples of contemporary Irish ingenuity. It means that Renvyle looks like an hotel and has the scale of an hotel, but feels more like a country house. It means that the food is cutting edge, and yet is also simple and unpretentious, earthy and agrestic, smartly sourced from excellent local artisan suppliers. It means that Renvyle feels traditional, yet is as modern as you need it to be. Reconciling all these seeming contradictions takes a particular form of genius, and these two genial blokes have it in spades. *Renvyle, County Galway + 353 95 43511 www.renvyle.com*

Kylemore Abbey

The restaurant and shops at Kylemore attract 350,000 visitors each year, making it the biggest tourist destination on the West Coast. The Benedictine nuns of the abbey still produce some chocolates. *Kylemore, County Galway + 353 95 41146 www.kylemoreabbeytourism.ie.*

Avoca

The Avoca crew are a class act, and their utter discrimination is as evident here on the West coast as in their Wicklow and Dublin heartland. *Letterfrack, County Galway + 353 95 41058 www.avoca.ie*

Rosleague Manor

Mark Foyle's house is one of the prettiest of all the Irish country houses. Pretty in pink, with the most to-die-for location and setting, it is a quintessential part of Connemara, fusing the elegant with the elemental in a sublime cocktail. *Letterfrack, County Galway + 353 95 41101 www.rosleague.com*

Above: Kylemore Abbey

The Connemara Hamper

The Connemara Hamper is just that: a little space, packed chock-a-block with lovely things from near, and from far. Like a good hamper, it unveils itself slowly, as you come to realise just how many things Eileen and Louise have managed to pack onto the shelves and into the deli. Superlative sandwiches and rolls to take away just solved your lunchtime dilemma. *Market Street, Clifden, County Galway + 353 95 21054 www.connemarahamper.com. Open daily.*

Dolphin Beach

In Dolphin Beach, the small details are all there: the comforting pot of tea and biscuits when you arrive; perfect beds with crisp linen; beautiful books to leaf through in the front room; home-made breads and jam; the warm welcome. Clodagh Foyle has innkeeping in her blood, and it shows. She effortlessly juggles a million household tasks, and yet is always ready with a smile. Dolphin is the house in which to truly unwind. *Lower Sky Road, Clifden, County Galway + 353 95-21204 www.dolphinbeachhouse.com*

Opposite: The Quay House

♪ Mallmore Country House

Siobhan Hardman has succeeded her parents and taken charge of the lovely Mallmore, though she still works alongside her Mum in running the house. It's a charming and quietly grand historic house, dating from the late 1700's, and five of the six rooms have terrific views of the garden and the bay. Breakfast features buttermilk pancakes with smoked salmon, French toast with bacon and maple syrup, and the traditional Irish breakfast has fresh eggs from their neighbour, whilst the preserves are made with Siobhan's own home-grown apples and fruit. It's only a mile outside Clifden, so not far to go to access the town's restaurants and bars. *Clifden, County Galway + 353 95 21460 www.mallmore.com*

⑂ Mitchell's Restaurant

it's not just the room that feels right in this busy Clifden destination: the service and the food in JJ Mitchell's restaurant enjoy a consistency that you don't expect in a busy tourist town like Clifden. A friend once described Mitchell's to us as 'the most consistent restaurant I know from visits over the last five years'. That is an incredible accolade, but the team here earn every word of it, and never make the mistake of resting on their laurels. Their people-pleasing dishes – fine fish and chips, a good chowder, crab with brown bread, good fish cakes, good lunchtime sandwiches – bring people back time and again at lunchtime, and while the evening menu is more extensive, the team show they are in full control with every plate sent out. *Market Street, Clifden, County Galway +353 95 21867 www.mitchellsrestaurantclifden.com. Open lunch and dinner.*

♪ Quay House

The thing about Paddy Foyle of Clifden's legendary Quay House is that he does everything... wrong. When he puts a set of plates, or a set of cloches to hang on a wall, for instance, he doesn't aim for them to be symmetrically arranged, the way the rest of us

would. He just fires them up there and when he's finished they look... incredible. Amazing. Perfect. And yet, wrong. Many years ago we described him as an 'iconoclast', but in retrospect we're not certain that was correct. Iconoclasts destroy, but Mr Foyle doesn't destroy: he just creates differently. He can see one room as a surrealist would see it, and another room will be formal, yet undershot with humour and wit. Whether you reckon he's an iconoclast or a maverick, let's agree that Paddy Foyle is probably the greatest interior designer in Ireland, and he is certainly the most unique. 'I remain in awe of the sheer exuberance and lightheartedness of these extraordinary interiors', the blogger Pamela Peterson wrote. What will also leave you in awe is the hospitality, the welcome and the cooking from Julia and her family. *Beach Rd, Clifden, County Galway + 353 95 21369 www.thequayhouse.com*

Sea Mist House

After the huge storms of winter 1998 tore the roof off her 175-year-old house, Sheila Griffin decided to remake and remodel, and to open Sea Mist as a guest Bed and Breakfast. Ms Griffin is humorous and wise, a great source of information about the town and the county, a designer with an expert eye for colour and compatibility, and the creator of particularly memorable breakfasts. With access to her own garden fruits, freshly-laid eggs and honey, she is leagues ahead of the average B&B, so what is a cliché in the hands of others – the traditional Irish breakfast, for example – feels freshly minted here, the quality of ingredients second-to-none. All told, the freshness and vitality that Sea Mist exudes is completely winning. *Clifden, County Galway + 353 95 21441 www.seamisthouse.com*

Local Food

The words 'Savage Beauty' have been bandied around to describe various locations - but the phrase was initially coined by Oscar Wilde, about Connemara. The national food of this region is **Connemara Hill Lamb**, a food which was awarded PGI status in 2007. Connemara Hill Lamb comes from a Blackfaced Horned Ewe, a rugged, adaptable animal that grazes on the particular grasses and sedges and heathers and is well suited to the sometimes punishing climate of these mountainous uplands.

57

Above: Connemara Smokehouse

Below and opposite: O'Dowd's Seafood Bar

Connemara Smokehouse

Bunowen Pier is at the edge of the earth, the end of the earth. To the west of Graham Robert's Connemara Smokehouse, which is housed in a stone building at the edge of Bunowen Pier, there is the Atlantic Ocean, and nothing else. A place so nakedly elemental is just the right place for Graham Roberts to weave his magic with smoked fish. The beech wood he uses for smoking his fish in the 1946 smoking kiln he works with allows for more subtlety than oak smoking, so the Connemara Smokehouse products are blessed with a grace and subtlety, an elusiveness, the merest touch of the beech smoke. And there are no shortcuts taken here: everything is done old school, by hand, by intuition, by experience.

The good news is that the smokehouse is also an economusée, so you can visit and see the artisan process as it plays out, from the filleting to the smoking to the packing. *Bunowen Pier, Ballyconneely, Clifden, County Galway +353 95 23739 www.smokehouse.ie*

Ballynahinch Castle

Patrick O'Flaherty and his team run one of the best operations in the west, and their castle is distinguished not just by great service and excellent cooking, but also by the fact that this is the most unpretentious castle on planet earth. It's a great destination, a few minutes' drive from the coast road, but be warned: as you make your way on the WAW, arriving here, walking in the door to see the always lit fire blazing in the hearth, may delay your plans to head further south or north on the route.

Ballynahinch is easy to enter, and hard to leave. A Connemara classic. *Recess, County Galway + 353 95 31006 www.ballynahinch-castle.com*

Angler's Return

'Not much has changed here over the year', writes Lynn Hill of the beautiful Angler's Return, one of the great Connemara hideaways. Part of that endearing old charm is the fact that Angler's Return is an 'unplugged' house: 'I still definitely keep it a TV-free zone', says Lynn, 'a house of peace and silent sounds, crackling fires and garden birdsong, but I have succumbed, reluctantly, to wi-fi for guests. I fought against it, keeping my computer hidden in the office, pretending that guests didn't need to contact their loved-ones, know the weather, check their Apps or their flights, but realised that everyone now has to be 'logged on' and 'linked-in'!!' Well, get those messages over fast, and get back to the crackling fires and the garden birdsong. *Toombeola, Roundstone, County Galway + 353 95 31091 www.anglersreturn.com.*

O'Dowd's Seafood Bar & Restaurant

Four generations of the O'Dowd family have rattled the pots and pans of this Connemara institution in beautiful Roundstone, acquiring both a national and international audience along the way. And they have acquired their legendary status by serving simple, consistent, tasty food – seafood gratin; poached salmon; smoked salmon pasta; beef and Guinness stew – both in the fantastic, classic bar and in the restaurant. The cooking here is just right, executed with classy confidence and a winning lack of pretention. It's splendid that they stay open all year, so even when the winter is in full flight outside, getting a seat by the fire and a pint of stout and a plate of gratinated oysters is just the thing. *Roundstone, County Galway + 353 95 35923 www.odowdsbar.com. Open lunch and dinner.*

6

Galway Bay

The poet Seamus Heaney described the three islands of Aran as 'stepping stones out of Europe', a precise and poetic sizing of the lonely trio's appearance on a map. There they rest, just a hop, a step and a jump away from Clare, from Galway and Connemara, alone together in the Atlantic, with New York to the west and the sallow gap that is Galway Bay opening away to the east.

Step out of Europe, onto the stones, and you are greeted with a surround of clean green sea and by limestone, limestone everywhere. Slate grey in colour, threaded here and there by green pastures, and trellised by mile after mile of dry stone walls. The writer Tim Robinson has described this eviscerated landscape: 'This bare, soluble limestone is a uniquely tender and memorious ground.... this land has provided its inhabitants – the Neolithic tomb-builders, the Celtic cashelore, the monastic architect, the fence-making grazier of all ages – with one material only, stone, which may fall, but still endures.'

If Aran is bare, Galway city is a blast of energy, a torrent of people. The City of Tribes is the only Irish city that was never conquered, and it feels that way to this day: it's a rebel place. Galway is a wild metropolis and, if that wildness gets in your blood and in your bones, you can find that you arrive here, mainline the energy, the artiness, the intimacy, and never again leave. The city doesn't just exude energy, it attracts energy, and so it's food and hospitality culture is stuffed with people who came here, promptly fell in love with the place, then opened up shop and got stuck into the business of feeding people, and making them happy.

Builin Blasta

Some cooks know how to get the flavours onto the plate, and J-me Peaker is one of those cooks. Whether he is baking a loaf of bread, dressing a pizza with smoked salmon, cherry tomatoes, cheddar cheese and rocket, finishing off the crisp pastry on a sausage roll or rustling up a bowl of chowder with breads or making one of his signature dressings or relishes, he always hits the taste target with the accuracy of an assassin.

Above: Builin Blasta

This simple tastiness – allied, it should be said, to a charming lack of pretension, and a lively, informal dining room with the best, chilled-out sounds you can hear – explains why Mr Peaker is a local hero, and why Builin Blasta is the destination that locals will insist you must try if you are anywhere near to Spiddal. The menu here never changes because no one will allow it to change, so every dish is a signature dish, and every dish is cooked by Mr Peaker. So, head to the rere of the craft village to enjoy an eclectic offering of dishes – filo tart of goat's cheese and smoked aubergine; pork and apple salad with crispy sage; chocolate and beetroot brownie – that all share one common aim: drop-dead deliciousness. Sublime. *Spiddal Craft & Design Studios, Spiddal, County Galway +353 91 558 559 www.spiddalcrafts.ie*

Connemara Coast Hotel

The Connemara Coast gleams like a jewel, and the staff are as good as it gets – polite; charming; assured; professional. You get a sense of welcome and warmth from the second you walk in the door, and the kitchen is meticulous. Owner Richard Sinnott is one of the greatest Irish hoteliers, and his staff match him every step of the way in fashioning a truly memorable destination. *Furbo, County Galway + 353 91 592108 www.connemaracoast.ie*

Donnelly's of Barna

Donnelly's is one of the classic West Coast pubs, a characterful collation of rooms right by the side of the road at Barna, where you will enjoy some really excellent cooking. They describe themselves as a landmark, and that's not an exaggertion. So, let's order up some hake with a garlic and herb crust, the fine haddock mornay, the monkfish with bacon and leeks, and all is good. *Barna, County Galway + 353 91 592 487 www.donnellysofbarna.com*

Mulberry's

James and Deirdre Cunningham have a stylish room in the centre of Barna and Mulberry's offers Mr Cunningham's creative take on modern Irish food – Gilligan's sirloin with smoked tarragon butter; shellfish pan with crab claws, mussels and prawns in tarragon cream; Roscommon beef cheek with grilled prawns; organic salmon with kale and bacon; scallops with dilisk and Savoy cabbage. You can also have a simpler, tapas-style menu in the wine bar. *Barna, County Galway + 353 91 592123 www.mulberrys.ie*

The Twelve Hotel

The Twelve, a groovy, colourful hotel at the junction in Barna, west of Galway city, is a fascinating place. It's as modern as all-get-out and yet... and yet it is utterly traditional in a uniquely Irish way. How so? It's because of the team who work with manager Fergus O'Halloran, who work in the old Irish way, which is to say: they look after you. They are patient, funny, generous, and unself-conscious. They make the experience of staying here special and, in the bar and restaurant (and their excellent pizzeria), you see this social genius at work at pell-mell pace. A key player in their success is chef Martin O'Donnell. Mr O'Donnell is an ambitious chef, and his cooking matches the colourful, modern palette of the hotel – Marty's mussels with baby mussel fritters; Connemara seatrout with poached oyster; scallops with McGeough's smoked sausages. *Barna Village, County Galway + 353 91 597000 www. thetwelvehotel.ie*

O'Grady's on the Pier

Mike O'Grady's end-of-pier restaurant is atmospheric and charming, and has been consistent and reliable for many years. Seafood is their signature, and the team like to riff on the classics to show their swerve: Clare Island salmon with smoked potato purée; plaice with Killary mussels, smoked tomato and chervil butter; silver hake with smoked paprika vermouth. There are dishes apart from fish and shellfish, of course, but those are the ones we go for. The restaurant has a sister establishment, Kirwan's Lane, in Galway city. *Seapoint, Barna, County Galway + 353 91 592223 www.ogradysonthepier.com. Open dinner.*

Pizza Dozzina

Dozzina made news locally when the two-and-a-half ton Napoliforni oven was manoeuvred into the lower ground floor kitchen and Connemara traffic was brought to a standstill. Today it looks as if Dozzina has always been there, and what is more, it always seems as if we Irish have put our fine ingredients on a pizza, because after all what better showcase could you get for some Connemara charcuterie, or some of our farmhouse cheeses. Each pizza is tossed by hand by a motivated, enthusiastic team, and Dozzina is a winner. *Barna Village, Galway, County Galway + 353 91 597012 www.thetwelvehotel.ie. Open lunch and dinner and takeaway.*

Local Food

Marion Roeleveld is one of the most gifted of modern cheesemakers, and her signature style in both of her **Killeen Farmhouse Cheese** Goudas is a liminal sweetness, and a clean, lactic purity. Ms Roeleveld works with both goat's and cow's milk, and also make Cais na Tire, a sheep's milk cheese. Modern Irish farmhouse cheesemaking doesn't get better than this. The aged cheeses, in particular, are masterful creations, and you will find them in Sheridan's Cheesemongers in the centre of Galway.

www.killeencheese.ie

Opposite: The Twelve Hotel and Pizza Dozzina

da Roberta, L'Osteria & Pizzeria

L'Osteria is the more formal restaurant sister of Salt-hill's popular da Roberta Pizzeria, and it's equally atmospheric and enjoyable. The food is effectively Italy's Greatest Hits: sea bass with potato crust; chicken wrapped in Parma ham; linguine with seafood. The pizzeria da Roberta is not devoted solely to pizzas – there are classic starters, pasta dishes, meat dishes and so on – but the pizzas and calzones are rock-steady good, and attract a fanatical following. It's manic, theatrical, and it's always brilliant fun. *157 & 161 Upper Salthill, Galway, County Galway 091-581111 (L'Osteria) 091-585808 (Pizzeria)– Open lunch and dinner.*

Gourmet Tart Company

We think the GTC in Salthill is one of the most beautifully designed eating spaces we have ever seen, reminiscent of Daylesford Organic in Notting Hill.Our editor, Eamon Barrett, writes: 'We arrived at twelve thirty for lunch and by one o'clock there wasn't a table to be had – always a sign that you're in good hands. The menu is cleverly simple: soup, sandwiches, salads and a small selection of hot food - but everything we ate was prepared with care and was tasty and satisfying. Leaving without trying some of the amazing cakes will be almost an impossibility. A superb operation that Salthill is extremely lucky to have.' *Salthill Upper, Galway, County Galway + 353 91 861667 www. gourmettartco.com. Open daily and early evening.*

Morton's of Galway

Eric Morton's store is one of the masterly pieces of culinary editing in Ireland. Mr Morton sells everything you need, and no more. He has the best of the best, and that's all he has. There is no rubbish here, no shelf fillers. Breads, vegetables, charcuterie, meat, a fantastic range of traiteur foods to take away, excellent wines. It's all here, beautifully arrayed and presented. A model enterprise. *Lower Salthill, Galway, County Galway + 353 91 522237 -www.mortonsofgalway.ie*

Norman Villa

Mark and Dee Keogh's beautiful house is one of Salthill's most famous destinations, and amongst the most stylish. They offer two rooms for B&B, as well as running an art gallery in the house. *86 Lower Salthill, Galway, County Galway + 353 91 521 131 www.normanvillagallery.com*

Oslo

Oslo is a great big enormodrome of a pub, at the seaside end of Salthill. Of most interest to visitors is their fine range of slickly named craft beers, from their Galway Bay Brewery: Strange Brew; Bay Ale; and Stormy Port. The beers are crisp and clean and well made, and they match up with the modern tasty food served in the bar – bangers and mash; steak burger; salmon and haddock fish cakes; beer-battered fish. Most of the Irish craft beers are also sold, as well as a great range of international brews. *Salthill, Galway, County Galway + 353 91 448 390 www.winefoodbeer.com*

The Royal Villa

The Chang family's Chinese restaurants are amongst the longest-established in Galway, and their Salthill restaurant is housed in the National Aquarium. The menus are modern and pan-Asian in style. *Salthill, Galway, County Galway + 353 91 580131 www.royalvilla.ie*

Salthill Traditional Fish and Chips

This traditional chipper is a local hero, thanks to serving good fish and chips, and taking time and patience to get their burgers and the other parts of the menu as good as they can possibly be.
Salthill, Galway, County Galway + 353 91 584 444. Open lunch and dinner.

Local Food

McGeough's butchers have been in business for more than forty years. Four decades in which father and son, Eamonn and James, have shown that they have no peers when it comes to being creative charcutiers. James McGeough's experiments with charcuterie have chiselled him a singular position in Irish butchering. His air-dried lamb, beef and pork and fantastic smoked sausages are well stocked throughout Galway city and county.

www.connemarafinefoods.ie

Aniar

Aniar is probably the greatest restaurant Galway has ever enjoyed. As a contrast to the incredible food, Aniar enjoys low-key simplicity: everything is quiet, the staff glide around the room, and there is even a baby seat. From an amuse of dehydrated cabbage crisp with black garlic and duck croquette, through to the most wonderful crab with zesty citrus notes, then onto fantastic scallops with peas and tissue-thin pork fat draped across them, each course is just one jaw dropper after another. Neck of pork with beetroot, and monkfish with barley and mussels sound simple, but they will bring conversation between you to a halt. At a recent dinner, the star of the evening was a beetroot and rosewater parfait with scorched meringue, described by a friend as 'possibly the finest dessert I have ever tasted', although a pear and sheep's milk yoghurt was also quite stunning. A restaurant without pretension, and one of the very best in Ireland.

53 Lower Dominick Street, Galway, County Galway + 353 91 535947 www.aniarrestaurant.ie Open dinner.

Anton's

A stone's throw from the Corrib, Anton O'Malley's little corner room on Father Griffin Road does the good thing. Everything they make and bake is wholesome, unpretentious, true and good. We like the calmness of the crew, and you don't find places like Anton's away from Galway, so settle in with a coffee and some buttermilk pancakes, or their hot tuna focaccia, check out the art on the wall, and mainline the culture. *12a Father Griffin Road, Galway, County Galway + 353 91 582067 www.antonscafe.com. Open daily.*

Ard Bia at Nimmos

Aoibheann McNamara and her team set benchmarks with everything they do – service; style; ambience; cooking; uniqueness; artistry. We don't use the term artistry casually: Ms McNamara and her crew are artists to their core. They just happen to produce stunningly delicious food, but what lies behind it is not just the instinct to cook, but the instinct to create, to create something striking, memorable, distinct, transformative; inspiring. Eating at Ard Bia is like taking part in a Happening: you, the customer, becomes part of the work of art that is the daily life of this extraordinary restaurant in this extraordinary city. *Spanish Arch, Long Walk, Galway, County Galway + 353 91 561 114 www.ardbia.com. Open lunch and dinner.*

Bierhaus

Bierhaus is a haven for beer heads, and offers the most amazing selection of craft beers. Lately, however, more folk are heading here for Paul and Frank's incredible sandwiches, including their classic pork banh-mi, their smoked mackerel Po'Boy, the three cheese grill, the smoked bacon BLT with fried potatoes, the tofu banh-mi. The sandwiches are unlike anything else in the city, and you'd have to be in New York or Barcelona to meet their equivalents. If you think that Irish pubs = ham sandwich and Guinness, then Bierhaus will blow your mind. *2 Henry Street, Galway, County Galway + 353 91 587 766 Open daily*

Opposite: Tigh Neachtain's Bar

Above: Brasserie on the Corner

Below: Cava Bodega

Opposite: Chi

Artisan

Matt Skeffington's Artisan is a small, long, upstairs room that they have decorated simply and appropriately, with bentwood chairs and strings of lights. The food is as simple and appropriate as the decor: boeuf bourguignon, baked salmon, and some thoughtful, artful sandwiches. *2 Quay Street, Galway, County Galway + 353 91 532655 www.artisangalway.com. Open lunch and dinner.*

Blakes Bar

The sister bar to Brasserie on the Corner has its own menus – carrot and coriander soup; Madras-style chicken and sweet potato curry; lamb stew with barley – and it's a typically characterful Galway pub. *25 Eglington Street, Galway, County Galway + 353 91 530053*

Brasserie on the Corner

Galway's Brasserie on the Corner shows just how to do excellent, middle-market food. Chef Joe Flaherty sources from the Best-in-the-West and, in doing so, he upends all your expectations. Deli boards are beautifully composed, organic salmon with sweet potato risotto is right on the money, and the cooking has an earthy tenor: good food cooked smartly and honestly. The staff are as sharp as the food and BOTC is a rare bird: a middle-market destination that serves its customers honestly and well. *Eglington Street, Galway, County Galway + 353 91 530333. www.brasseriegalway.com. Open lunch and dinner.*

Cava Bodega

In Cava Bodega, expect the unexpected, like earthy chicken hearts and a piquant chorizo sauce, or a sweet little rib-eye and foie gras burger in a crunchy brioche bun, or pork neck with migas, morcilla and piquillo peppers. Cava is a Tardis-like space, both upstairs and downstairs, but it's the big Iberian flavours that the kitchen conjures up that are outsize here, and Jp McMahon and his team are on a roll these days, firing out smashing food to delight everyone with an appetite. The staff are amongst the very best, and the list of Spanish sherries and wines is sensational. *1 Middle Street, Galway, County Galway + 353 91 539884 www.cavarestaurant.ie. Open dinner.*

Chi

Andy Bandara and Catherine O'Brien operate two Chi outlets, the city centre branch in Middle Street and the take-away branch in Westside. Their dishes span the Orient, with influences and specialities from Malaysia, Singapore, Thailand, Vietnam and China, so you can run the gamut from egg fried rice to roast duck and king prawn soup hor fun with beansprouts, Asian greens and tofu. The Middle Street room is simple and homey. *2 Middle Street, Galway, & Unit 4, Westside Enterprise Park, Westside, Galway, County Galway chigalway.com + 353 91 861687 Open evenings for dinner and take-away.*

7 Cross Street

Paris has lots of little hotels where you walk through a single narrow door, then down a narrow entrance to a little reception desk and, having checked in, you climb steep stairs to the warren of little bedrooms. Olivia O'Reilly's No 7 Cross Street is one of those hotels – the narrow doorway on the street, the narrow hall, the tiny reception space, the tiny rooms, the city centre location, the bustle and noise of the city right outside your window. So, No 7 suits us perfectly, and if you like petite rooms – let's call them intimate – and cheek-by-jowl eating, then you will love this chic space on Cross Street. They also offer a rental house just across the river. *7 Cross Street, Galway, County Galway + 353 91 530100 www.7crossstreet.com*

Local Food

Jennie Browne has pretty well the whole of Galway slathering over her scrummy **Goodness Cakes**. Her pictures on Facebook get shared hundreds of times and thousands attend the Bakefest which she organises each autumn. 'My aim is to inspire and educate people about the value of baking. The little changes each home can make can make a difference and recreate traditions that have been passed down through generations', she writes about Bakefest, and her cakes cook up both inspiration and goodness in every mouthful.

www.goodness.ie

Dela

Dela is one of the new arrivals in Galway's restaurant quarter, opened by Joe and Margaret Bohan who had previously worked out in County Mayo. They like the concept of sharing plates – an 'indoor picnic' is their lovely turn of phrase – so there are charcuterie and cheese and seafood plates, alongside smaller plates of Connemara mussels or goat's cheese salad. Evening menus have brilliantly sourced ingredients and are more conventional, so you can enjoy Rossaveal scallops with pork belly and Brady's Hereford steak with portobello mushrooms. *51 Lower Dominick Street, Galway + 353 91 449252 www.dela.ie. Open lunch, brunch, dinner.*

Delight

Paula Lawrence's health café is at the Kingfisher Club in Renmore, in the east of the city. Their focus is on health-giving, energising food, so there are power salads and detoxing juices, smart sandwiches and good toasted bagels. It's lovely to see a destination that balances health and satisfaction so implicitly and successfully in its food. *Renmore Avenue, Galway, County Galway + 353 91 761 466 www.delight.ie. Open daily.*

Dail Bar

The Dail is one of the classic Galway pubs, perenially busy with a young crowd, and it's a valuable port of call in the city as it serves good food from breakfast through to dinner. The name doesn't reference Ireland's parliament, however: it means a place where people meet to discuss and debate. *42-44 Middle Street, Galway, County Galway + 353 91 563 777 www.thedailbar.com.*

Front Door

A hugely popular Galway pub, particularly with sports fans, and with ambitious cooking – check out the Herterich's trio of pork special, for example, with braised pork belly, apple and coriander sausage and black pudding and spring onion croquette. *High Street, Galway, County Galway + 353 91 563 757 www.frontdoorpub.com.*

Goya's

Emer Murray's status as the best baker in Galway has never been challenged in more than two decades. When Ms Murray first opened her little store on Shop Street, she was immediately the best. In her hip Kirwan's Lane café and shop, she remains the best, a patissier of infinite precision, exactitude and accomplishment. Nothing comes out of the kitchen at Goya's – from the simplest sandwich to the most mellifluously ethereal cake – unless it is the best it can possibly be. Goya's is endlessly inspiring. *2/3 Kirwans Lane, Galway, County Galway, + 353 91 567010 www.goyas.ie. Open day time.*

Opposite: Goodness Cakes

Dunmanus
€25/kg

Smoked Gubbeen

Region: Schull, Co. Cork
Milk: Cow's
Rennet: Traditional
Maturity: 4 Weeks +
Producer: Ferguson Family

Waxed rind, firm lactic paste with mildly smoked
after flavours. Giana and Tom Ferguson have been
making Gubbeen since 1980. It is oak-smoked by
their son Fingal in his purpose built smokehouse.

SHERIDANS
CHEESEMONGERS

€24.60
per
kg

Griffin's Bakery

Saturday morning, and the queue to buy breads at Griffin's is winding down Shop Street. Jimmy Griffin's bakery is no mere food store. Instead, it is a temple of good things, and we all come here to pledge fealty to Mr Griffin's devotion to making beautiful things to eat. Mr Griffin hasn't just continued the family business. Instead, he has super-charged it, steadily broadening the list of breads and cakes, running a superb tea rooms, and yet never losing their focus on the fact that 'Bread is not bread unless it is made by an artisan bakery.' *21 Shop Street, Galway, County Galway + 353 91 563683 www.griffinsbakery.com. Open day time.*

The Heron's Rest

There is a heron. He's called Jack. In Galway, Heron's Rest means just that: the B&B where the heron — Jack — comes to rest. You couldn't make it up. Mind you, you could hardly make Sorcha Mulloy up, either. There is no more meticulous hostess in Ireland. But she's funky, too, and she creates a breakfast that has no parallel in Ireland. Last time we started with beautiful fruit salad with goji berries and yogurt, then pearl barley porridge with poached cinnamon pears and honeyed dates. We felt like we could have taken to the skies, just like Jack. *16a Longwalk, Spanish Arch, Galway, County Galway + 353 86 337 9343 www.theheronsrest.com.*

Opposite: Sheridan's Cheesemongers

Opposite: Tigh Neachtain's Bar

The House Hotel

The House is a good boutique hotel, with excellent rooms and staff who work hard and take their job seriously. It is popular with hen parties, mind, but we're okay with that. *Lower Merchants Road, Latin Quarter, Galway, County Galway + 353 91 538900 www.thehouse.ie*

The Huntsman

The Huntsman offers a text-book lesson in how to do middle-market food as well as it can be done. By middle-market we mean cooking that is affordable, democratic and delicious, food that appeals to young and old, food that is great on a quiet Monday and perfect on a raucous Saturday, and that is what you will enjoy in this extraordinarily successful bar and restaurant. On a recent visit for dinner we enjoyed warm duck confit terrine; black kale and goat's cheese spring roll; classic homemade chicken goujons; a perfect beef burger, and then a dessert of orange cheesecake with vanilla ice cream and homemade honeycomb. Every dish was right on the money, and made all the better by terrific service from engaging and witty staff. Lovely rooms upstairs to rest your head also. *164 College Road, Galway, County Galway + 353 91 562849 www.huntsmaninn.com. Open breakfast, lunch and dinner.*

Above: The Huntsman

Kai Café + Restaurant

In Kai, Jess Murphy shows that there is nothing she can't cook to its zenith of flavour and texture, no ingredient that doesn't make her mind race with a furious creativity - Silke's halloumi; goat's curd; Brady's striploin; sea buckthorn and apple sea beet hogget chops; her own labneh with dukkah; West coast crab with Green Goddess dressing. The food in Kai is not just elemental, it is instinctual, it broaches no argument in its total confidence and philosophical sureness. For many food lovers, Kai is their favourite restaurant not just in Galway, but in Ireland. David Murphy runs the room superbly, and value is excellent. *Sea Road, Galway, County Galway + 353 91 526003 www.kaicaferestaurant.com. Open lunch and dinner.*

Kappa Ya

Kappa-ya is a Celtic Japanese restaurant and, if that sounds like some kind of crazy fusion, then that is exactly what it is. Junichi Yoshiyagawa interprets Celtic ingredients through the prism of his Japanese culinary skills, and the result is unlike anything you will find anywhere else The room is tiny and when they do the magic, there is

nowhere else like it. *4 Middle Street Mews, Galway, County Galway + 353 91 865930. Open daily.*

Kettle of Fish

The Kettle of Fish is the city outpost of a fine fish and chip shop that originally opened in Gort, south of the city. They make splendid fish and chips – dry, crisp, hot, flavourful, light, beautifully executed and a real demonstration of the fryer's art. Everything is cooked to order, and it's a commonplace to hear people say that Kettle of Fish make the best fish and chips. *4 Lower Cross Street, Galway, County Galway + 353 91 569881. Open lunch til late.*

The Kitchen @ Galway City Museum

A confession: when we find ourselves in The Kitchen, we can never make up our mind. Why? Because we want to eat everything. We want the aubergine and chickpea curry with curried lime yogurt. We want the citrus and coriander cured salmon with caper and horseradish potato salad. We want the hasselback sweet potatoes (who else does that!) with buttermilk chicken. We want the chilli caramel pork shoulder banh-mi. The team here are infinitely cool, and they cook the coolest grub, in that uniquely cool Galway style. *Spanish Parade, Galway, County Galway + 353 91 534883 www.galwaycitymuseum.ie. Open daily.*

Above: Kai Café + Restaurant

Galway Atelier

'Dramatic simplicity' is a phrase used by **Cloon Keen Atelier** to describe their products, and scents of Cloon Keen are a way of capturing everything that is lovely about this county and bringing it home to enjoy. Their fragrances, when experienced through the medium of liquid soaps or scented candles, are generous, powerful and superbly crafted.

3 Kirwans Lane, Galway + 353 91 565 746 www.cloonkeenatelier.com.

Opposite: The Malt House
Below: McCambridge's

The Malt House

Is there another restaurant team that tries as hard as the crew in Mary and Paul's Malt House? These guys and girls put body and soul into their work, they give it 110% all the time, every time, and their effort makes for a thunderously pleasing destination. What is perhaps most striking is the fact that customers love the Malt House to bits: actually, the guys and girls eating here aren't customers, they are devotees, they are disciples, and we understand their faith. The cooking is delicious, the service is fantastic, and the totality of the experience of eating here is one of the highlights of Galway. *Olde Malt Mall, High Street, Galway, County Galway + 353 91 567866 www.themalthouse.ie. Open lunch and dinner.*

Massimo

Jp McMahon of Aniar and Cava Bodega does the food in Massimo, and the food is every bit as good and creative as that pedigree would lead you to expect. *William Street, Galway, County Galway + 353 91 582239 www.eatgalway.com. Food served lunch and dinner.*

McCambridge's

You need to hunt for the big words to describe McCambridge's of Galway. Ostensibly, it's a grocery shop, with a restaurant upstairs. But it's actually a bazaar of good things, a cornucopia of delicious delights. At each point of the store, something singular and seductive is waiting for you – superb wines; brilliant sandwiches; great savouries; sublime coffees; artisan meats; agrestic breads. Everything Natalie McCambridge and her family have chosen to grace their shelves is worth the detour, everything is characterful, real and life-improving. The wine bar and café upstairs is one of the great new destinations in the city, and it is worth the wait to get a table. *38/39 Shop Street, Galway, County Galway + 353 91 562259 www.mccambridges.com. Open day time and early evening.*

McDonagh's Seafood House

No one was the slightest bit surprised when *The Irish Times* loudly roared their approval of Galway's legendary McDonagh's, when the newspaper polled its readers as to which fish and chip shop was the best in Ireland. Their fish restaurant is just as beloved as the chipper, and just as busy: the room is perennially packed – just like the

chip shop – and you come to McDonagh's for fresh fish, fish that they source and cook correctly, so get ready to enjoy fish dishes that they send it out with confidence, consistency, and charm. *22 Quay Street, Galway, County Galway + 353 91 565001 www.mcdonaghs.net. Restaurant open dinner, Fish and Chip bar open lunch and dinner.*

Martine's Quay Street Wine Bar

Martine put a hip, smart new facade on her hip, smart wine bar in 2012, but behind the new surface, this Galway institution does what it does the way it has always done it: cooking nice food, making people happy, ensuring they come back time and time again, and doing everything with a smile. Martine and her team could coast on the tourist trade, but they don't: every day they make it new, and we salute their energy. *21 Quay Street, Galway, County Galway + 353 91 565662 www.winebar.ie. Open for dinner weekly, lunch and dinner weekends.*

Maxwell's Restaurant

Paul O'Meara's bistro is friendly and fun and the cooking is spot on: tasty food with something that suits all ages and which is very affordable. *Williamsgate Street, Galway, County Galway + 353 91 568974 www.maxwellsrestaurant.ie. Open lunch and dinner.*

Local Food

Jorg Muller is an advocate of Goethian science, so his search as a tea blender is on understanding how the plants and leaves he uses actually work, and catching them and their essential properties at their optimum. His handsome **Solaris Teas** are his search for the answer. We are devoted to them, their vibrancy, their cleanness and health-giving properties.

www.solarisbotanicals.com

Oscar's

Oscar's latest innovation, where the weekly fixed price menu is available all evening, has seen the room packed with happy punters who share a plate of little amuse-gueules to begin, then choose the day's fresh fish dish, or a Hereford beef sirloin steak, or the day's vegetarian dish. At 15 euro, this is a steal for such clever cooking, and it's another example of how Michael O'Meara is steadily working his way towards an ever more impressive simplicity. *22 Upper Dominick Street, Galway, County Galway + 353 91 582180 www. oscarsbistro.ie. Open dinner.*

Petit Delice

Bread lovers will tell you that the baguette baked here in the little Petit Delice is the best in town. It is indeed very good, but so is everything else they make, and the few chairs and tables at the rere of the store make for an excellent spot for taking tea and nice sweet treats. Petit, yes, and perfectly formd and quite delicious. *7 Mainguard Street, Galway, County Galway + 353 91 500751. Open day time.*

The Pie Maker

You can have your pie sitting in The Pie Maker if you can get a seat, and then the turkey and ham or the spinach and feta comes served with mash, mushy peas and gravy or with salad. If the sun is shining you can take your sausage in veal gravy pie or your roast beef pie away and go sit down by the River Corrib. *10 Cross Street, Galway, County Galway + 353 91 513141. Open day time.*

Sheridans Cheesemongers and Winebar

Sheridan's is unique. On the ground floor is the best cheese shop in Ireland. Upstairs is the best winebar in Ireland with the best wines you can buy in Ireland and delicious cheese and charcuterie plates to accompany them. But it's not just the wines and the cheeses that make Sheridan's special: it's the atmosphere, the ambience, the staff, the electricity that happens when you put a bunch of the most interesting people in a city into one room. It's not a wine bar: it's a wine salon. *Yard Street, Galway, County Galway + 353 91 564829 (shop), + 353 91 564832 (wine bar) www.sheridanscheesemongers.com.*

37 West

'Healthy is the new sexy' is Gill Carroll's guiding slogan in the funky 37 West, and judging by the success the café has enjoyed in its first year, Galwegians agree. Gill uses the excellent Les Petits Douceurs artisan breads, makes smashing breakfasts – don't miss the breakfast burrito – and whilst there is a healthy focus to everything, that doesn't mean there aren't big, satisfying flavours here, it just means it's smart cooking. *37 Lower Newcastle, Galway, County Galway + 353 91 524122 www.37west.com. Open daily.*

Tigh Neachtain

Galway has lots of good pubs, but it's hard to beat Neachtain's for that sepia-tinted, low-lit, always-4pm-in-the-afternoon feeling. One of the great classic pubs. *17 Cross Street, Galway, County Galway + 353 91 568820 www.tighneachtain.com.*

Tulsi

A tiny room with a big menu that delivers excellent Indian cooking is the Tulsi signature. It's modest and simple, and the service is wonderful, the cooking always consistent and enlivening. *3 Buttermilk Walk, Middle Street, Galway, County Galway + 353 91 564831 www.tulsigalway.com. Open lunch and dinner.*

Local Specialit

Les Petites Douceurs are up early in the morning to make specialist, artisan baguettes and Viennoiseries, and you can find them in good restaurants and markets in the County.

Opposite: Sheridan's Cheesemongers and Wine Bar
Above: Petit Delice

The Salt House

There are 150 bottled artisan beers for sale in this beautiful bar, and some 23 craft beers and ales and stouts on tap, so you step in the door and basically step into Beer Heaven. The crew are purist – there are no beers whatsoever from the corporate brewers – but they aren't didactic about it, so if you are bewildered by the amazing

choice, simply ask what they recommend and hitch a ride to Beer Heaven. And be careful with their Of Foam and Fury Double IPA: it's a monster! *Ravens Terrace, Galway, County Galway + 353 91 441550. Open pub hours.*

Vina Mara

Eileen Feeney has overseen Vina Mara for almost a dozen years now, and has exhibited superlative professionalism all that time. With chef Rachel Lynch heading up the kitchen team, the cooking is wonderfully moreish – chicken with chorizo and chestnut stuffing; venison sausages with mash and thyme gravy; hake with pesto and sautéed greens; lemon and rhubarb tart. Vina Mara also offers great value. *19 Middle Street, Galway, County Galway + 353 91 561610 www.vinamara.com. Open lunch and dinner.*

Wa Café

Everything you love about Japanese food – the use of colour; the sense of proportion; the deep wisdom; the quiet focus on nutrition; the enlivening hit of umami flavours – can be found in the small, intimate space that is Yoshimi Hayakawa's Wa Café. Ms Hayakawa and her crew prepare beautiful food – simple, soulful, respectful – and serve it with grace. *13 New Dock Street, Galway, County Galway + 353 91 895850 www.wacafe.net. Open daily to early evening.*

Opposite: Wa Café
Above: The Salt House

Basilico

Careful sourcing from stellar suppliers such as Toonsbridge mozzarella, Pigs on the Green, Gannet Fishmongers, Brady's butchers of Athenry and Friendly Farmer pastured free-range chicken signals that Paolo Sabatini and his team are super serious about their work in Basilico, and this meticulous sourcing of Irish and Italian ingredients allied to imaginative and professional cooking explains the success they have enjoyed since opening. Their ability to offer beloved Italian specialities in Basilico — porchetta; octopus bruschetta; chestnut and potato gnocchi; porcini tortelloni; lobster ragu in arborio risotto with saffron; Sicilian cannoli — alongside the straight-ahead menu they offer in the House Bistro of the Coach House Hotel, and to serve excellent pizzas, is one of the great feats of culinary discipline. *Main Street, Oranmore, County Galway + 353 91 483693 www.basilicorestaurant.ie. Open breakfast, lunch and dinner.*

Kate's Place

At the top of the escalator in the Orantown Centre you will find Kate Wright's sweet little café. Ms Wright was a staple of the McKennas' Guides when she ran the Cobblestone Café in the city. Her little room in Oranmore is bright and girly, with a small counter of delicious things begging you to come and taste them — bakewells; apple pies; Tunisian orange cake — and lots of tables and chairs out front on the concourse. In the evening, Kate conducts various cookery classes, so come along and learn from an experienced expert. *1st floor, Orantown Centre, Oranmore, County Galway + 353 86 6066494 www.galwaycookeryclassses.com*

Claire's Tearooms

Stone walled. Richly furnished. Elegant china. A classy bit of retail. Oh, it would be great to have Claire Walsh's singular, special tearooms and shop as your local, rather than experiencing it as a roadside stop in Clarinbridge when heading south or north on the WAW. Ms Walsh's Tearooms is a little oasis of civility and culture, with dainty, vibrant cooking, and a singular aesthetic that makes you feel better as soon as you step in the door. Give yourself plenty of time to linger here. *Clarinbridge, County Galway + 353 91 776606. Open daily.*

Moran's Oyster Cottage

Yes, Moran's is an international tourism staple, with photographs of this pretty water's edge cottage a fixture of every guide book, but don't worry about that. It's famous because it's good, because it's reliable and professional, and because they know what they do well and they do it as well as they can. Catherine Moran is the seventh generation of the family to run this beautiful waterside bar. They do some lovely things – oysters and brown bread, chowders, fish platters – and with a pint of creamy stout, you will wish to be nowhere else. *The Weir, Kilcolgan, County Galway + 353 91 796 113 www.moransoystercottage.com. Open lunch and dinner.*

The Tide Full Inn

Marianne and her husband, Joseph, serve good honest Italian food in this lovely old pub in the centre of town. They keep things nice and tight, with a short list of simple starters, a few pasta dishes and a few main courses. Their signature pizzas are not just good, they are funny: the Berlusconi! the Bastardo! the Tide Full Out! the Drunk! Reading about them is almost as much fun as eating them. And don't miss the fine baking – Rocky Road; orange and polenta cake. A super place, with grown-up cooking that is a quiet treat.
Main Street, Kinvara, County Galway + 353 91 637400 www.thetidefullinn.com. Open lunch and dinner.

Kinvara Market

Music plays, chickens (such handsome chickens!) cluck, people ramble from stall to stall in the walled garden, shopping and eating and chatting and admiring the chickens, and there is everything from Sri Lankan curries to seaweed to local honey to handsome sweaters. Kinvara is a lovely, left-field market: do not miss it!

Behind Johnston's Hall, Main Street, Kinvara, Friday 10am

Opposite: Moran's Oyster Cottage

Opposite and below:
Ruairi and Marie-Thérèse
de Blacam, Inis Meáin
Restaurant and Suites

Local Food

Look out for
**Cáis Gabhair
Árann** a new Goat's
Cheese from the Aran
Islands made by Gabriel
and Orla. They make a
soft cheese flavoured
with Dillisk seaweed,
and a Gouda-style hard
cheese from their herd
of Nubian and Saanen
goats.

Inis Meáin Restaurant and Suites

We don't want to get all Zen on you, but if you come to beautiful Inis Meain and stay and eat at Ruairi and Marie-Thérèse de Blacam's gorgeous restaurant and suites, what you will experience is: Oneness. This extraordinary place brings everything that is special about these islands together – the light, the stone, the sea, the colours, the food, the sense of time. It all becomes One. The cooking is simple, perfect: island vegetable soup; dressed crab; seafood pot with tomato and fennel; saddle of lamb with peppers; apple tart and crème anglaise. The calmness of the food, the fact that it is grown and reared and caught outside the door, the charming service, is almost overwhelming. *Inis Meain, Aran Islands + 353 86 8266026*
www.inismeain.com

An Dún

Potatoes from the garden. Fresh mackerel. Carrageen pudding for dessert, another lovely day as you enjoy dinner in Teresa Faherty's simple B&B and restaurant. Mrs Faherty has been looking after guests here since 1989, and doing so with grace and sympathy. *Inis Meain, Aran Islands + 353 99 73047*
www.inismeainaccommodation.com

Kilmurvey House

To understand Aran requires one thing: time. So,

book yourself into Treasa and Bertie's lovely house. Swim in Kilmurvey Bay. Trek the island. Explore Dun Aengus. Relax in the bars of Kilronan. Enjoy Treasa's stupendous breakfasts. Enjoy Bertie's hospitality. Kilmurvey House is your portal for these pleasures. *Kilmurvey, Inis Mór, Aran Islands + 353 99 61218*
www.kilmurveyhouse.com.

7
The Flaggy Shore, the Burren, the Cliffs of Moher

The seizing and shifting of the ages has given us not just the appearance of the Burren in County Clare, but also the secret of the Burren. It looks naked, but is profuse with life. It looks invincible but, in fact, it is being eroded and eaten all the time, every second.

'Boireann may be a rocky place, but water, not rock, is the essence of The Burren' writes E. Charles Nelson in his book on the wildflowers of the area. 'Water brought the rock into existence; aeons later frozen and running waters fashioned the karst landscape. Water moreover, will be The Burren's ultimate destroyer.'

Here is another sign of the hidden Burren, for underneath the stone is an underworld of caves. The play between limestone and water which produces the karst means that the water of the Burren runs underground. There are many turloughs, places where the water, mysteriously, will be one day present and the next day disappeared.

Take a tour through the honeycombed tunnels of the Aillwee caves and one sees the decisive, tireless destruction carved out by the subterranean water, in the powerful falls of the streams as they pummel the soft stone, how all of this magnificent natural intricacy will, one day, be worn to oblivion. Underneath the karst, that grey, schismed pavement with its secret wealth of flora, the stone is being steadily, ceaselessly disemboweled.

And this is the ultimate secret of the Burren. It exists as it is because it is balanced, at the end of the land and the edge of the sea, made of rock that was once eroded from above and is now being eroded from below. It is barren in appearance, but uniquely fertile.

Opposite: Burren Smokehouse

Linnalla Ice Cream

Wild lavender and garlic ice cream, anyone? Someone did ask Roger and Brid Fahy to make them an ice cream with these flavours once, so these guys are up for any challenge. They have seized the challenge of becoming artisan ice cream makers with gusto, expanding their range, creating new flavours, opening a shop in New Quay (which you have to visit), and winning acclaim. *New Quay, County Clare + 353 65707 8167 www.linnallaicecream.ie*

Above: Wild Honey Inn

Mount Vernon

Mount Vernon is a house of true beauty. One of its secrets is that it shows the importance of travel, as everywhere you look an artefact collected from Asia, Africa, South America, or elsewhere is to be found in exactly the right place within the room. Yet it's not cluttered, it's almost as if all the ornaments ran into the house and chose their own space. The food is simply delightful: fish broth with prawns, lemon and dill nourishes the soul. Halibut, juicy to the bone and well cooked, with new potatoes and colourful, well-cooked vegetables is what simple, honest, home cooking is about. Mount Vernon fits beautifully with the wild Flaggy Shore – Ally and Mark have made a special place here. *Flaggy Shore, New Quay, County Clare + 353 65-707 8126 www.mountvernon.ie*

Burren Beef & Lamb

Lamb and beef reared in the Burren benefits from a unique Burren grass-based diet distinctive of its upland limestone terrain. There is today a positive awareness of this special landscape, and farmers and producers are actively involved in conservation with strict self-imposed codes of practice. There is a huge pride in Burren food that starts on the farm, and ends at the butcher's counter or in the local restaurants.

The Russell Gallery

We are big fans of the lovely wines Stefania Russell imports from her native Italy, served along with coffees and organic teas and scones and smoked salmon and antipasto plates, in the aesthetic comfort of Stefania and Andy's delightful gallery, in gorgeous New Quay. Mrs Russell selects her featured artists well, and Mr Russell's raku pottery is sublime. *New Quay, County Clare + 353 65 7078185 www.russellgallery.net*

Aillwee Cave

Everything about Aillwee Cave is superbly managed. The design, the structure of the tours, the charm of the staff, the good food in the café, the hawk walk and birds of prey area and, of course, their rather special shop. You shop here for their own Burren gold cheese, but over the years their range has increased exponentially, so now you come for the cheeses, and the fudge, and the ice cream and much more. *Ballyvaughan, County Clare + 353 65 707 7036 www.aillweecave.ie*

L'Arco

The Quinn family offer good cottage accommodation in Ballyvaughan, and also run the craft shop, in addition to their L'Arco restaurant. L'Arco is a solid, mid-market destination, with all of Italy's greatest culinary hits. *Main Street, Ballyvaughan, County Clare + 353 65 7083900 www.burrenrestaurant.com*

An Fear Gorta

'I don't think I've ever seen anything like it!' said Eamon Barrett when he walked into Jane O'Donoghue's tea rooms and spied the display of delights set out on the big table in this lovely room. Cakes with fruit, chocolate, coffee, cheese, caramel, toffee – you name it. If the baking is fantastic, the service matches it, making for one of the great Ballyvaughan destinations. That's Stephen Spielberg over there, isn't it? Yeah, thought so. *Pier Road, Ballyvaughan, County Clare + 353 65 7077023 www.tearoomsballyvaughan.com*

Co Clare Cheeses

St Tola goat's milk cheese is probably the best known of the County Clare cheeses, but as you travel the WAW look out also for the fine **Cratloe Hills,** made with sheep's milk, hunt down the hard-to-find **Kilshanny** goudas, which rarely get beyond the county borders, head to the Aillwee Caves to find Ben Johnson's **Burren Gold** cheeses, and if you can get your hands on a piece of Lucy Hayes' aged cheddar-style cheese, **Mount Callan,** then it's going to be a very good day indeed.

Wild Sea Veg

'Hand harvested, hand packed', says Gerard Talty, explaining the stunning quality of **Wild Irish Sea Veg.** Mr Talty might have also pointed out that four generations of the family have harvested vegetables from the sea, so experience and knowing discrimination play their part. These are outstanding products, benchmark examples of each variety, all beautifully packaged, and there is no easier nor better way to get vital, mineral-rich sea vegetables into your diet.

www.wildirishseaveg.com

Opposite: Gerard Talty, Wild Irish Sea Veg

Burren Fine Food & Wine
Don't miss Cathleen's roadside operation as you climb or descend Corkscrew Hill. Not only is the cooking really fine, but service is gracious and sincere. So, a pizza for you, some lemon drizzle cake for me and are we happy? More than. Quite lovely. *Corkscrew Hill Road, Ballyvaughan, County Clare + 353 65 7077046 www.burrenwine.ie. Open day time.*

Gregan's Castle
'A splurge worth every euro' was how Frank Bruni of *The New York Times* described Gregan's Castle after an overnight stay. Frank is dead right. Gregan's is worth every cent that you will spend here, because it is an inspiring place. Everything in Gregan's Castle seems to float with the ease and grace of a note of music moving through air, delighting and somehow wondrous. The setting; the architecture; the design; the aesthetic; the inspired cooking and the welcome all conjoin to make for one of the most sensual experiences in Irish hospitality, and there are times here when you can feel you are somehow embedded in a work of art, rather than simply staying at an hotel. Freddy's design plays an enormous part in creating this effect, for here is a house where every object and every objet is in exactly the right place. Simon's hospitality is impeccable, and chef David Hurley's cooking is a thing of beauty – don't leave without buying several jars of his amazing dressings and sauces. Worth every euro, because there is nowhere like it. *Ballyvaughan, County Clare + 353 65 7077005 www.gregans.ie*

O'Lochlainn's Bar
O'Lochlainn's is one of the most beautiful bars in Ireland. Intimate, zen-like, handsome, and with a jaw-dropping selection of whiskeys, it is probably the Irish pub we would most like to be locked into. Time stands still from the second you walk through the narrow green doors. *Ballyvaughan, County Clare + 353 65 7077006 www.irishwhiskeybar.com*

The Burren Smokehouse

Brigitta Curtin's Burren Smokehouse is one of the great European smokehouses, with some of the best smoked fish you can possibly eat, so do make this little detour off the WAW into Lisdoonvarna and treat yourself. *Kincora Road, Lisdoonvarna, County Clare + 353 65 7074432 www.burrensmokehouse.ie*

The Roadside Tavern

Peter Curtin's pub is a west coast classic, and the arrival of his own beers, which Peter created and began brewing in 2011, has made a great pub even greater. Lovely music sessions, too, and nice, proper cooking. *Kincora Road, Lisdoonvarna, County Clare + 353 65 7074084 www.roadsidetavern.ie*

Above: The Roadside Tavern

Sheedy's Hotel

The Sheedy family's hotel is a modest delight, a place where everything is made from scratch, and where the hospitality matches the excellence of the cooking. When you stay here you understand what a true 'family-run' hotel is, and how precious a thing it is. *Lisdoonvarna, County Clare + 353 65 7074026 www.sheedys.com*

Wild Honey Inn

Aidan and Kate's Wild Honey Inn has enjoyed spectacular success over the last five years, as befits a wonderful destination with inspired cooking and excellent, inexpensive rooms. The Wild Honey may seem like little more than a simple, classic bar, but the cooking will knock your socks off: this is some of the best food in the West, and not just at dinnertime but at breakfast time also. *Kincora Road, Lisdoonvarna + 353 65 7074300 www.wildhoneyinn.com*

Local Food

As defining a part of the county as the Cliffs of Moher or Willie Clancy, the **Clare Jam Company** is an archetypal artisan company, its distinctiveness due to the diligence and vivid creativity of David and Vera. Beautiful jams, traditionally made, and the views from the shop will take your breath away.

www.clarejam.ie

♪ Cullinan's Restaurant & Guest House

James and Carol Cullinan's restaurant with rooms in the centre of Doolin offers good cooking – sea bream with smoked salmon and spring onion risotto; marinated Burren lamb with a spring roll filled with confit shank of lamb, and good breakfasts will set you up for that promising day ahead. *Doolin, County Clare + 353 65 7074183 www.cullinansdoolin.com.*

♪ Hotel Doolin

There is energy in Hotel Doolin, in the cooking: crisp tripe with belly of pork; leeks and rhubarb with salmon; pickled samphire with Burren Smokehouse smoked salmon. This sort of creativity shows what they are doing here – they are avoiding the clichés that make so many hotels humdrum, avoiding the by-the-rulebook mantra that makes staff in hotels so dissatisfied. And all the while they are hosting craft beer festivals, writing festivals, music festivals. Stay here and you catch that energy. *Ballyvoe, Doolin, County Clare + 353 65 7074111 www.hoteldoolin.ie*

⸙ Fabiola's Patisserie & Café

Fabiola Tombo's patisserie is only excellent. Ms Tombo worked just up the road at the great Gregan's Castle as a pastry chef before setting out her stall in Doolin in 2011, and her baking made an instant splash with locals.

Most of the baking is sweet, and expert, such as her great hazelnut sponge with chocolate ganache, but savoury local foods do sneak deliciously into muffins with St Tola goat's cheese and spring onions. Not to be missed. *Ballyvoe, Doolin, County Clare + 353 86 6602582. Open daytime.*

Roadford House

Frank and Marian show exactly how to run a restaurant with rooms. A genuine welcome, some simple, crisp accommodation, and some wowee! cooking. Put them together, and you have an archetype of the coaching inn, the welcome retreat for the WAW traveller. The cooking is direct and elemental, and unwaveringly precise: this food hits the target, so a dish like St Tola goat's cheese parfait with brick pastry, fig, beetroot, hazelnuts and a truffle honey dressing is a perfect example of wham-bam! sweetness and textures allayed together to stunning effect. You see it again in chicken 3 ways, which comes with red pepper, spinach and a wild mushroom cream. And Yotam Ottolenghi would just love to be able to cook amazing puddings like lemon meringue sundae, or deconstructed cheesecake. *Doolin, County Clare + 353 65 7075050 www.roadfordrestaurant.com. Open dinner.*

Vasco

Ross and Karen have wandered the world, and they bring experience and influences back home to Fanore and to the menu at Vasco: Burren lamb in a Tangier sauce; braised Burren kid goat pie; beef massaman curry; smoked mackerel and rocket tart; wild garlic pesto and walnut pasta; carrot and walnut cake. The value is good, the room is funky, and the left-field vibe is pure County Clare. *Fanore, County Clare + 353 65 7076020 www.vasco.ie. Open lunch and dinner.*

Opposite: Doolin Hotel
Above: Fabiola's Patisserie & Café

The Cliffs of Moher

Sometimes there are so many visitors at the beautiful Cliffs of Moher that it can almost seem as if it's compulsory to have it on your itinerary. It isn't compulsory to visit, but it is advisable, for the cliffs are truly stunning, and the visitor centre is only excellent.

8

Liscannor Bay
to Loop Head

The myth that locals will tell you when you are on the Loop Head is that there is a hidden city – Cill Stuifín – which was submerged in an earthquake some time ago, round about the fifth century.

Only Loop Head could claim to have a hidden, submerged city as part of the Wild Atlantic Way. They'd never think of that down in Dingle, or in West Cork.

Hidden, it may be. Submerged, it may be. But, in the style in which you come to expect things in south County Clare, it seems that Cill Stuifín can be glimpsed, every seven years.

Except, you don't want to gaze at it, because doing so will bring you bad luck.

Only Loop Head could claim to offer you the most spectacular, incredible vision known to man, but then tell you not to bother looking at it.

This sort of phantasmagorical craic, this audaciousness, is one of the reasons so many of us love Loop Head. It's different. It's mythic, and they make their own myths.

WILD ATLANTIC WAY

Vaughan's Anchor Inn

If you wanted to summarise Denis Vaughan's cooking in a single dish, you could scarcely do better than 'Sean Digger's lobster, sautéed foie gras, apple, pistachio, tomato.' It's all there: the local ingredients cooked with care, the lush, rich counterpoint that the liver gives to the shellfish, then the flavour games with unexpected ingredients as the apple, pistachio and tomato offer flavour tangents to the supremely luxe ingredients. This is the kind of thing you get at Vaughan's, rich imaginative food that comes as a surprise when you first walk into the bar and the dining room. You might have been expecting fish and chips and mushy peas, and suddenly you are offered "Cod in a 9-year-old starter batter, chips steamed then fried in beef dripping (hooray for beef dripping!), homemade tartare sauce, pea purée." This sense of surprise, the juxtaposition of a traditional Irish pub with this resolutely modernist food, is part of the joy of Vaughan's, and it has won Mr Vaughan a devoted audience, who relish the food, and relish the value, and also relish being able to get a pint of stout. Prepare to be surprised. *Main Street, Liscannor, County Clare + 353 65 7081548 www.vaughans.ie. Open lunch and dinner.*

Vaughan Lodge

Multi-millionaire Chip O'Hare stayed at Vaughan Lodge as part of a golfing trip with a bunch of similarly affluent buddies during summer 2011. Kathy Sheridan, of *The Irish Times*, asked Chip what he reckoned of Michael and Maria Vaughan's work: 'Vaughan Lodge was excellent', wrote Chip. 'Obviously new and neat and clean. Superb food and service was cordial and first rate. Michael was a great host and hard worker. We had a dinner there on our last night with the guys from Lahinch and it was lovely.' Well, that's the million-dollar American market taken care of for the foreseeable future. Michael and Maria are consummate professionals, which makes Vaughan's a wonderful place to stay and to eat. *Ennistymon Road, Lahinch, County Clare + 353 65 7081111 www.vaughanlodge.ie*

Moy House

Moy House is handsome, it's distinctive, it's singular. It's a house that unwinds its charms slowly, a destination that soon captivates you. Eamon Barrett found that: 'The more time I spent there, reading, looking out to the rough sea, helping myself to Power's 12-year-old whiskey from the honesty bar, the more I liked it. In the evening, there were slippers and candles lighting. We had our own turf fire in the room, for goodness sake! At breakfast the next morning there was truly superb service and an excellent breakfast of scrambled egg with mushroom accompanied by really good brown bread. Staff were excellent, and nothing we asked for was too much trouble.' *Lahinch, County Clare + 353 65 708 2800 www.moyhouse.com*

O'Looneys on the Prom

O'Looneys took a fearful hammering from the winter storms of 2014, but by Easter the bar and Green's coffee shop were back in business, good news for Lahinch. *The Prom, Lahinch, County Clare + 353 65 708 1414 www.olooneys.ie. Open lunch and dinner.*

Morrisseys

Hugh McNally has transformed this lovely pub in Doonbeg from a traditional Irish bar into a svelte restaurant with rooms, yet he has managed to keep the ambience of the old place, where four generations of the Morrissey family have plied their trade. The cooking is modern and informal – chicken Caesar salad; Angus beef burger; salmon and cod fish cake; homemade scampi with tartare sauce – food that you can relax with and there are also excellent rooms upstairs. *Doonbeg, County Clare + 353 65 905 5304 www.morrisseysdoonbeg.com. Open lunch and dinner.*

Local Food

Considine's Bread
Every town in Ireland used to have a bakery like Considine's of Kilrush. But the others have vanished whilst Considine's has thrived. The guys bake in the back of the shop and sell their breads from the shop, as well as having a van on the road to deliver to local businesses in south Clare. They have survived because they bake simply wonderful breads.

Above: Images of Ché, who stayed in The Strand Hotel, Kilkee when travelling the Wild Atlantic Way.

Diamond Rocks

The views from the Diamond Rocks Café out over Kilkee Bay are simply stunning. Whilst it's a lovely stop-off as you walk the coastal path, it's also a fine destination in its own right. And do check out the Richard Harris statue! *West End, Kilkee, County Clare + 353 86 3721063 www.diamondrockscafe.com. Open day time.*

McNamara's

There is a small bakery corner in this Early till Late convenience store, that is devoted to the baking of Deirdre Daly. Deirdre is a specialist and talented patissier, so grab these treats for your picnic. She also manages the food in the Kilkee Golf club during high season. *11 O'Connell Street, Kilkee, County Clare + 353 65 905 6075. Open daily.*

Murphy Blacks

Cillian and Mary are two of the major players in the Loop Head food community, and Mary's cooking showcases the great fish and pristine ingredients of the region with stunning success – mussels steamed with cider and shallots; Loop Head crab tart; Atlantic cod with curried leeks and saffron cream; cannelloni of plaice; seafood zarzuela. There are smart, modern carnivorous choices – shank of lamb in 8 Degrees red ale; Kelly's Kilrush sirloin – and Cillian looks after everyone with great charm. A charming restaurant. *The Square, Kilkee, County Clare + 353 65 905 6854. Open dinner.*

Naughton's Bar

Elaine and Robert offer some fine, tasty cooking in Naughton's, with a focus on fish and shellfish, abetted by a selection of meat dishes. They wisely keep things simple, and focus on getting excellent ingredients and showing them proper culinary respect. *45 O'Curry Street, Kilkee, County Clare + 353 65 905 6597 www. naughtonsbar.com. Open dinner.*

The Pantry Shop & Bakery

Imelda's café and bakery can seem to be the very epicentre of Kilkee on a busy summer day, with everyone calling in to eat breakfast, buy breads and cakes, sit around over a lazy lunch or read the paper over a cup of coffee. We suspect many Kilkee holidaymakers are in and out of The Pantry several times a day, starting with a berry dazzler and a wee

Irish in the morning, then coronation chicken salad for lunch, and a cup of tea and a slice of carrot cake as evening draws in. *O'Curry Street, Kilkee , County Clare + 353 65 905 6576 www.thepantrykilkee.com*

Stella Maris

Stella Maris is a treasurable old resort hotel, and Anne Haugh and her family do a brilliant job of looking after their guests. The rooms are cosy, the cooking is very, very good, and the sense that this is an hotel for the community is precious. It's also a completely unpretentious place, where everyone does their job as well as they can. *O'Connell Street, Kilkee, County Clare + 353 65 9056455 www.stellamarishotel.com*

The Strand

Caroline Byrne really enjoyed Johnny and Caroline Redmond's cooking and hospitality in The Strand. "Lovely food, and a stunning view of the bay", says Caroline. That lovely food is honest and true – Carrigaholt crab claws; Parmesan chicken; Donegal silver salmon; chocolate cola cake. Six nice rooms upstairs are advising you that it's okay to have another digestif. Che Guevara stayed here back in 1961, don't you know. True. *Kilkee, County Clare + 353 65 9056177 www.thestrandkilkee.com. Restaurant open dinner.*

Above: Stella Maris

The Long Dock

Think of the highest standards you can discover in Irish food, then take a drive way down the Loop Head to Carrigaholt, park on the big wide street and marvel as Tony Lynch shows how he can match those standards, dish by dish. The brown bread is superlative; the chowder is a classic; the fried fish is stunning; the fish pie is sheer class. The fact that you are enjoying this cooking in a great pub that is traditional yet utterly of-the-moment, with good music, a roaring fire, and great service, means the Long Dock is truly a standard setter in south west Clare. Imelda Lynch marshals the room with ease, and the Long Dock is a classic. *Carrigaholt, County Clare +353 65 9058106 www.thelongdock.com. Open lunch and dinner.*

Above: The Long Dock

Loop Head Lighthouse

The lighthouse at the tip of Loop Head offers spectacular holiday accommodation, and can be rented from the Irish Landmark Trust. *Loop Head, County Clare + 353 1 6704733 www.irishlandmark.com.*

Purecamping

Purecamping is an eco-campsite which offers both pre-erected bell tents, or a wild camping experience for those who want a more remote experience. Yoga classes available on site. *Querrin, County Clare + 353 65 9057953 www.purecamping.ie*

Kerry Head to the Dingle Peninsula

In Kerry, beauty is all before you, but it is fleeting, a magical illusion that pulses and vanishes, then re-appears, rearranged. Around the Ring the light will spangle magically on the sea, then change to coat the waves with grey and subdue them, so suddenly they seem as smooth as velvet. After the rains come the illusory rainbows, sometimes so harshly coloured that they appear to be flames of light shooting from the land.

The kaleidoscope of colours and sensations changes every instant, and one can gaze simultaneously at a valley smothered by rain and cloud and, to east or west, find a bay dappled in pools of sunlight and bright with colour. The effect is entrancing, but also enlivening. Kerry air seems super-charged, invigorating, filled with energy. Up the Reeks or around the ring, you find this crazy energy, which the local dialect, a blur of singing vowels, echoes.

WILD ATLANTIC WAY

Rigney's Farm

It's rare to get a chance to stay on a working farm that specialises in rare-breed animals, so here is your chance. Caroline and Joe Rigney have a cosy B&B, and for breakfast you eat the sausages, rashers and puddings they produce themselves from their own much-loved herd. *Curragh-chase, Kilcornan, County Limerick + 353 87 2834754* www.rigneysfarm.com.

Restaurant 1826 Adare

It's a short detour into Adare, but worth the trip to see one of the prettiest villages in Ireland and, just as important, to eat Wade Murphy's cooking in 1826, for here is a chef at the top of his game. The understated nature of everything in 1826 is delightful, and the cooking is serene, mature and utterly delicious. *Main Street, Adare, County Limerick + 353 61 396004 www.1826adare.ie Open dinner.*

Wild Geese

If Adare is the prettiest village, then The Wild Geese is surely the prettiest restaurant. David Foley's cooking is intricate, but beautifully realised, and service from Julie is as good as it gets. *Rose Cottage, Adare, County Limerick + 353 61 396451 www.thewild-geese.com. Open dinner and Sun lunch.*

John R's

Just off the Tarbert ferry and need a good cup of coffee? Then the detour into pretty Listowel will take you to John R's, where Pierce Walsh and his team will look after you with aplomb. Do note that Mr Walsh also offers some excellent self-catering accommodation. *70 Church Street, Listowel, County Kerry + 353 68 21249 www.johnrs.com*

Above: Restaurant 1826 Adare

Sundaes Ice Cream Parlour
Ballybunion is golfer territory, but for food lovers it's where you come to get a bumper ice cream, and maybe a doughnut and a cup of coffee, from Joanna McCarthy's festive shop. *Main Street, Ballybunion, County Kerry + 353 86 0523089. Open daily.*

D'Arcy's
Rosemary and Helena are assiduous in using local foods in this pretty restaurant, particularly meats from their own butcher's shop. *Barracks Lane, Tralee, County Kerry + 353 71 94625 www.darcysbistro.com. Open dinner*

Above, below, opposite and preceding page:
Rigney's Farm

Kingdom Food & Wine
Pat and Maeve's shop is a treasure trove of good speciality foods and some excellent foods-to-go, so turn up at Oakpark for good coffees and freshly made sandwiches. *Oakpark, Tralee, County Kerry + 353 66 7118562 www.kingdomstore.ie. Open daily.*

Manna
Claire and Thomas run the most splendid organic store here on Strand Street, so if you have a picnic planned for somewhere along the WAW, then you need to head in to Manna for smashing organic foods from local producers. A great store. *Island of Geese, Strand Street, Tralee, County Kerry + 353 66 7125699 www.mannaorganicstore.ie. Open daily.*

Mary-Anne's Tea Rooms
What could be nicer than taking tea in Mary-Anne's, with a warm fire blazing and china cups and tiers of cupcakes and hot chocolate with marshmallows for the young ones. *17 Denny Street, Tralee, County Kerry + 353 87 6241837 Open daily.*

Quinlan's Seafoods

The Quinlan family have their own fleet of boats to catch their fish, so the fish they offer is as fresh as it can be. And after you have selected what fillet you would like to eat they have expert fish fryers to serve you perfect fish and chips and other excellent seafood dishes. Smart and slick and very clever indeed. *The Mall, Tralee, County Kerry + 353 66 7123998. Open daily.*

The Roast House

They have their own on-site coffee roastery in the Roast House, set in the lovely terrace of Denny Street, so it's the place not just for that good cup of Joe, but also for some funky lunchtime sandwiches and modern cooking such as lamb tagine and home-made burger with smoked Gubbeen cheese. Nice room, and the bar is a nice spot to sit with your iPad. *3 Denny Street, Tralee, County Kerry + 353 66 7181011 www.theroasthouse.ie. Open daily, weekend dinner.*

Spa Seafoods

Spa Seafoods has the best fish cookery in this part of the country, along with amazing views over the Dingle peninsula from the upstairs dining room. It's a short journey out from Tralee, but it's a trip every-one is happy to make to enjoy fish cookery of this quality. If you just want a snack, then there are stools and tables downstairs where you can grab a bowl of chowder, and the shop sells excellent artisan foods. *The Spa, Tralee, County Kerry + 353 66 7136901 www.spaseafoods.com. Open lunch & dinner.*

Louis Mulcahy, Caifé na Caolóige

Louis Mulcahy is one of Ireland's most famous potters and, like the man himself, there is artistic discrimination evident in everything the kitchen sends out, and it makes Caifé na Caolóige a vital destination on any Slea Head and Wild Atlantic Way tour. And when you consider that lots of the vegetables and leaves have come from no further than their own raised beds and other local plots and polytunnels, and most everything else is sourced from the peninsula, you know you are getting the true taste of the Dingle peninsula. If you can leave without buying a gorgeous piece of Mr Mulcahy's pottery, then you are made of sterner stuff than us. *Clogher Strand, Slea Head, County Kerry + 353 66 9156229 www.louismulcahy.com open day time.*

Gorman's Clifftop House

Quite how Vincent and Sile Gorman manage to maintain such a productive herb and vegetable garden, here in this guesthouse and restaurant at the edge of Smerwick Harbour, we don't quite know. But their fresh leaves and herbs add mightily to Vincent's classic cooking, bringing colour and contrast to the culinary canvas in Gorman's. Great comfort, great views. *Glaise Bheag, Ballydavid, Dingle, County Kerry + 353 66 9155162 www.gormans-clifftophouse.com. Open dinner.*

Craft Brewery

The **West Kerry Brewery** is Europe's most westerly micro-brewery, operating from Bric's Pub, on the Slea Head Drive. If ever a trio of beers deserved to have a sea salty tang to them, it's the coastal trio Béal Bán, the Cul Dorcha and the Carrig Dubh.

www.westkerrybrewery.ie

Left: John R's

Local Speciality

The **Dingle Distillery** is the first distillery created to fashion a new whiskey to be purpose built in Ireland in 200 years. Owned by the dynamic Porterhouse Brewing Company of Dublin, the first spirit for the whiskey was laid down in December 2012. When it is ready, the whiskey will be a five year old, triple pot-stilled single malt. Believe it or not, but at one time there were 1,200 distilleries scattered throughout the island of Ireland. Today, like artisan beer making, which suffered a long decline in Ireland before coming back with astonishing vigour in the last five years, artisanal distilling is again dynamic, with some twenty applications for distilleries having been lodged in recent times. Meantime, whilst waiting for the Dingle whiskey, do try the fine Dingle Original Gin and Dingle pot still Vodka: they help to pass the time.

www.dingledistillery.ie

Ashe's Bar

A simple thing happens when you walk into Sinéad and Thomas's bar: you don't want to leave. You may have only come in for a quick drink or a quick bite to eat, but we'll bet you change your plans very fast, and have another drink, and another plate of something delicious. Sure, the night is young, and how often nowadays do you find yourself in a classic pub like Ashe's, a pub with that inimitable, out-of-time character, and with excellent cooking. Nice simple rooms upstairs also. *Main Street, Dingle, County Kerry + 353 66 9150989 www.ashesbar.ie. Open lunch & dinner.*

Beile le Cheile

Blogger, cupcake-maker, marketeer and teacher Sharon Ni Chonchuir has opened this upstairs café in the courtyard in the centre of Dingle, and it's a simple and profound showcase for this warm-hearted perfectionist. *Upstairs in Dick Mack's Yard, Dingle, County Kerry + 353 87 7119647 www.beilelecheile.com. Open daytime.*

Castlewood

Just how much work does it take to maintain a house at the pitch-perfect level that Brian and Helen manage at Dingle's iconic Castlewood House? Every time you visit the house looks freshly painted: all of it! Everything gleams. The result is one of the best places to stay in Ireland, and one of the very best breakfasts you can eat, not just in Ireland but, we reckon, that you could eat anywhere in the world. *The Wood, Dingle, County Kerry + 353 66 9152788 www.castlewooddingle.com*

Right: Castlewood

Chart House

Charming is a word that doesn't suit many modern places to eat, but the Chart House is pure charm. Partly this is due to the wonderful service, partly to the almost domestic nature of the design, partly to the fact that the cooking is graciously modest, whilst being never other than professionally precise. And, the vegetables they serve here are out of this world: you won't taste a better potato in Kerry. *The Mall, Dingle, County Kerry + 353 66 915 2255 www.thecharthousedingle.com*

Above & Below: The Chart House

Dingle Reel Fish Co

Mark Grealy's fish and chip shop is one of the best in Ireland. The best fish from the harbour and the best, driest chips are delivered by a masterly cook who takes his calling seriously. Worth the drive to Dingle. *Holy Ground, Dingle, County Kerry + 353 66 915 1713. Open lunch and dinner.*

Emlagh House

Emlagh is a beautiful, serenely comfortable house that has featured in our annual 100 Best Places to Stay in Ireland book ever since it opened.

It's a place where everything conspires to gratify your senses - the tactility of the tableware, the sweep of the dining room windows and their view out onto Dingle Bay, the gorgeous art works that dot the house and which ache to emulate the drama of the restless light that plays on the hills above the town. Breakfasts are superb. *Dingle, County Kerry + 353 66 9152345 www.emlaghhouse.com*

Fish at the Marina

OK, so I'm having the seared tuna burger with black olive relish and chips and you're having the organic salmon fillet with gnocchi, spinach, tomato and basil, and my aren't we having a lovely time here in Alex Barr's place on the Marina. *Marina Buildings, Dingle, County Kerry + 353 86 378 8584. Open day time.*

Above: Emlagh House

Garden Cafe

Sheila Egan brings in all the good things from all the good produce from the good people in and around Dingle, and then serves them with charm and care. Meet you here for a Dingle Dog. *Green Street, Dingle, County Kerry + 353 87 7815126 www.thegarden-cafedingle.eu. Open day time.*

Global Village

Over the last fifteen years, Martin Bealin has honed his vision of Global Village, utilising foods from the peninsula and growing his own vegetables and herbs according to biodynamic principles. And so, in each dish, you can sense the deep nature, the impact of the sun and moon, the photosynthesis, the miracle of the things we eat. The dishes read simple – crab and cognac bisque; hake with chorizo; john dory with Dingle Bay prawns – but the flavours are endless, fathomless. *Upper Main Street, Dingle, County Kerry + 353 66 915 2325 www.globalvillage.com. Open dinner.*

Goat Street Bistro

'Slow food and fast service'. Can there be a higher aspiration in the world of food than to achieve those twin aims? But that is what Ed and Laurence achieve in the funky Goat Street Bistro, and they do it in a splendidly personal way. Customers tend to use expressions like 'new age' or 'could be in San Francisco' to describe the ambience and the creatively atypical cooking of the GSB. But, in fact, when you think about it, it's pure Dingle, pure West Kerry: people doing things according to their philosophies and their culinary culture, and doing it as well as they possibly can. *Main Street, Dingle, County Kerry + 353 66 915 2770 www.goatstreetcafe.com Open lunch & dinner.*

Greenmount
The Curran family have been beacons of hospitality since they opened Greenmount House in 1977, and if you ask anyone who has stayed in the family's stylish house to explain the particular appeal of this Dingle icon, you are likely to be told that it is the handmade nature of so much of what they do. Breakfast, in particular, with its fresh handmade breads, with the lovely handmade preserves, the delectable poached fruits, and freshly cooked hot dishes, offers a masterclass in the art of breakfast. *Upper John Street, Dingle, County Kerry + 353 66 9151414 www.greenmounthouse.ie*

Heatons
Cameron, Nuala and David Heaton seem able to read their guests' minds, so you will have scarcely made a request for something or other before they have it sorted. Their hospitality is only mighty, and the water's edge location is perfect. *The Wood, Dingle, County Kerry + 353 66 9152288 www.heatonsdingle.com*

Local Food

Jerry Kennedy is one of the pre-eminent Irish butchers, a master of the craft whose skills with rearing, sourcing and preparing meats underpin the food culture of the town. Mr Kennedy is particularly known for offering lamb reared on the Blasket Islands, where the shepherd is Donncha O'Ceileachair and where, as Donncha says, "the sheep are grazing on land that was never ploughed, so there is a nice mixture of grassland and heather." The **Blasket lamb** is unique, but then so is the Dingle Peninsula lamb which Jerry sources from a small network of farms on the peninsula, and equally superb is the beef from Jerry's own farm. It's all great.

Idás

Kevin Murphy earned a mighty reputation as a creative cook when working in Ballydavid, north of Dingle. The move into town for Idás will win a whole new audience for this gifted chef. Mr Murphy is an artist by training, and it shows: there is a painterly quality to his food that delights even before you eat it. He works wonders with fish and shellfish, and his crabbouleh is a don't miss! dish. Pretty amazing potatoes, too. *The Bull's Head, John Street, Dingle, County Kerry + 353 83 1036973*

Local Food

Kerry, and Dingle in particular have a long tradition of making pies. **Piog Pies**, in Dingle carry on the tradition with a wonderful array of pastries available throughout the peninsula. Look out for them in local shops and markets.

The Little Cheese Shop

Maja Binder is a cheesemaker who also runs a cheese shop: now, that's being qualified for your job. TLCS is a wonderful place to find wonderful cheeses in mint condition, as well as great foods and – hungry traveller alert! – some really crackingly desirable sandwiches for lunch. Don't miss this Dingle gem. *Grey's Lane, Dingle, County Kerry + 353 87 6255788 www.thelittlecheeseshop. net*

Milltown House

Milltown has one of the nicest locations of all the Dingle houses we feature, and under the new ownership of Stephen McPhilemy and Patrick Wade it is once again reasserting its status as one of the best places to stay on the peninsula. *Milltown, Dingle, County Kerry + 353 83 1477363 www.milltownhouse.com*

Murphy's Ice Cream

The original Murphy's ice cream store in Dingle remains a place with a unique ambience, and it has been one of the pivotal players in the culinary renaissance of Dingle that has seen the town rocket to pre-eminence, in particular when their annual food festival takes over the entire town in October. To say that the Murphy brothers make ice cream is to say that Horowitz played the piano. Better to say that they express their creativity, via the medium of ice cream. The coffees are amazing also, and the staff are as good as it gets. *Strand Street, Dingle, County Kerry + 353 66 9152644 www.murphysicecream.ie*

Opposite: Maja Binder at the Little Cheese Shop

Above: Out of the Blue

Below: On The Wild Side

Out of the Blue

If Tim Mason had a tenner for everytime the fish cookery in OOTB has been described as 'amazing', then he could retire and take it easy. Lucky us that Mr Mason didn't need anything other than a tiny budget, a tiny shack-like room and a dedicated team to open this brilliant, revolutionary, fishy adventure. They only cook the catch of the day, and they cook it superbly, and pair it with some of the best wines you will find. *Waterside, Dingle, County Kerry + 353 66 9150811 www.outoftheblue.ie. Open lunch and dinner.*

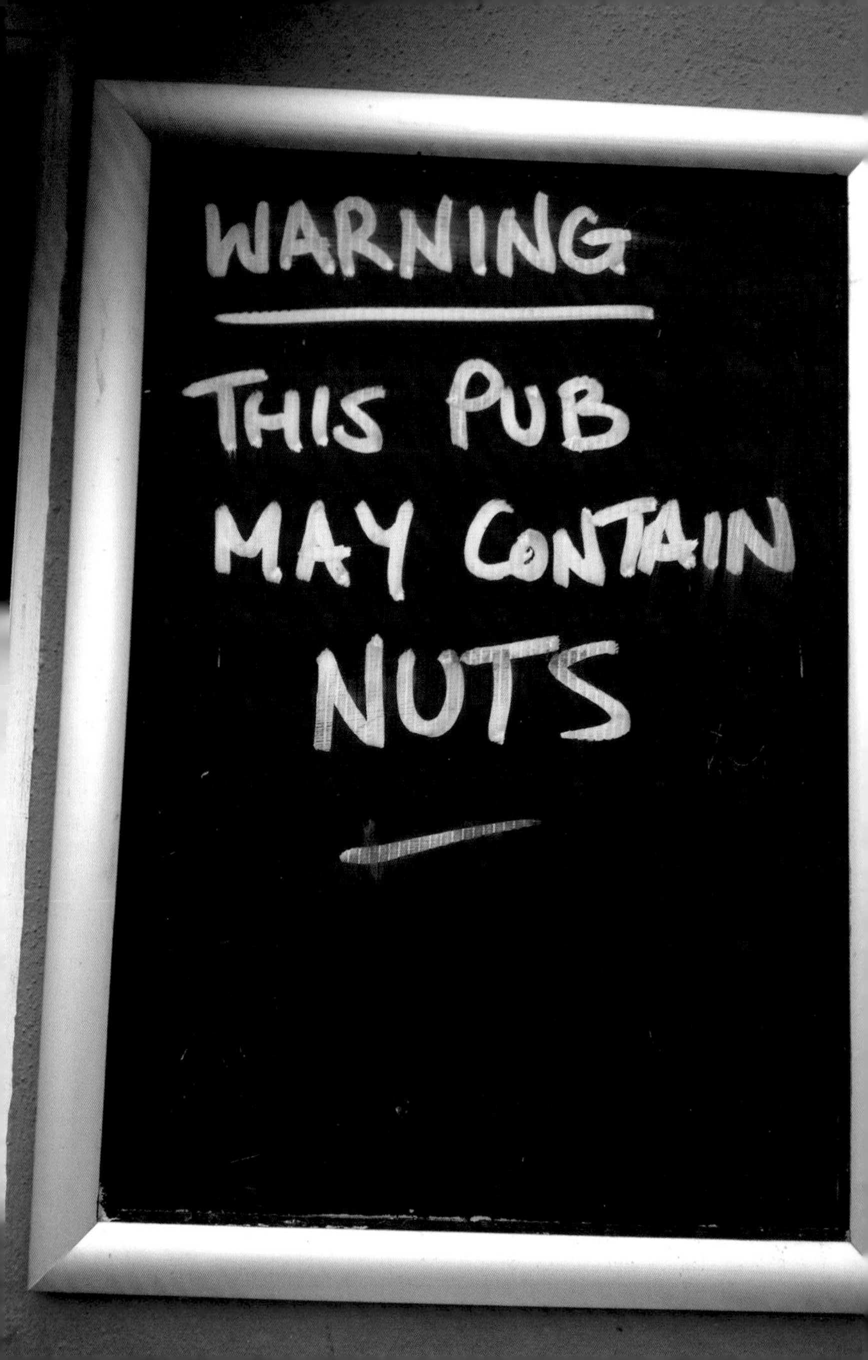
WARNING
THIS PUB
MAY CONTAIN
NUTS

South Pole Inn

When Antartic explorer Tom Crean retired after his adventures with Ernest Shackleton, he bought a pub in County Kerry. This is the pub, which is still as he named it 'The South Pole' – a place he never reached other than here in Anascaul. Call in for a pint and a sandwich and honour the life of this legendary Irishman. *Lower Main Street, Anascaul, County Kerry + 353 66 915 7388*

The Phoenix

'Rising from the side of a busy road just beyond Inch beach, is the wonderland that is Lorna Tyther's baby. Pull in and park your car and you'll soon forget about everything in the outside world.' That's the sort of instant effect Lorna and Billy Tyther's vegetarian guesthouse and restaurant, The Phoenix, tends to have on people. You pitch up here and the world vanishes. In its place arises The Phoenix, a quixotic demi-monde of inspired vegetarian cooking, belly-dancing and hippy-dippy hard work from the proprietors that ensures you will have a wonderful time. Sleep in a horse-drawn caravan if you can. *Shanahill East, Castlemaine, County Kerry + 353 66 9766284 www.thephoenix-restaurant.ie*

Milltown Market

Mary O'Riordan's Organic Store is a one-stop-organic supermarket. Everything you need is here, from the best local organic vegetables to wines to cheeses to fruits to books and including smashing gardening gear from the best specialists in Ireland.

And as you would expect from an idealistic and community-minded person, prices in Mary's Organic Store are very keen indeed. *Milltown, County Kerry + 353 66 9767869 www.milltownorganicstore.com*

Local Food

Ashe's Annascaul Black Pudding Co.

Thomas Ashe makes one of the most distinctive of the Kerry black puddings, and you will find it served in various ways in local restaurants in and around Dingle and further field. Thomas also produces some fine rashers and sausages for your breakfast table.

www.annascaulblackpudding.com

Above and Opposite: The South Pole Inn

10
The Ring
of Kerry

The most singular thing about Kerry, aside perhaps from the confident but not unpleasing pride of the locals, is the character of the light that washes over the county. At times it can seem to be purest monochrome, with sheets of celluloid silver light dissecting the hob-black tones that cover the hills. Then, with a sweep of wind that is announced by a cannon-fire rumble through the valleys, it will change to become peat-dark and gun-metal grey, and the hills will appear to be backlit, like some stage set or a post-modern painted landscape. The sea will dance with threatening dark washes devoid of colour, a lick of white foam fringing the waves, whilst on the land the light will fade to softer, natural shades.

It is an uncanny theatre of non-colours, and you try to explain away the curiousness of it all by reference to how far west the county is slung, how deeply sunk in the Atlantic ocean so much of it is. But this won't somehow convince you that the weird and singular quality of the light isn't just another aspect of the mysticism which can seem so readily believable in County Kerry. The soft mists with the promising threat of what hides behind them, the swirling fogs that further inoculate the light, the sense that a prospect of simple abandonment could lie just around the corner. You might find yourself here and just decide to stay, simple as that.

WILD
ATLANTIC
WAY

Valentia Ice-cream

Unhomogenised milk, buttermilk, yogurts with fruit, sorbets and numerous varieties of ice cream are the proud products that Joe and Caroline Daly make from the milk of their herd of friesians. It would be hard to better the quality of milk from a herd grazing on these windswept, sea salt spattered pastures. The milk and ice creams are pure tasting and delicious, and one senses that a search for purity – they wisely disdain homogenisation, for example – is what animates the Dalys. Don't miss their lovely dairy products, and do try to find the time to visit the ice cream booth at the farm itself.

www.valentiadairy.com

Nick's
Nick's is a step back in time, to the time of red banquettes, white tablecloths, carpets and fireplaces, bentwood chairs and kindly ladies in charge of service. For which we say: Hurrah! So, decide whether you want to eat in the bar or the restaurant, then order up the classics – prawn and monkfish thermidor; grilled lobster; rack of Kerry lamb with fondant potato; Dover sole with lemon butter sauce. *Lwr Bridge Street, Killorglin, County Kerry + 353 66 9761219. www.nicks.ie. Open dinner.*

Sol y Sombra
A tapas bar and music venue in a deconsecrated Church of Ireland? Only in Kerry, that's for sure. Cliodhna Foley's inspired adventure is so off the wall that it takes your breath away. You can even have your wedding reception here: now, what a day that would be! But, even if you haven't popped the question, the foods and wines in Sol y Sombra are reason to come here, and return here – bacon and egg bechamel croquettes; suckling pig; sausage with apple marmalade – and don't miss the wonderful sherries. *The Old Church of Ireland, Killorglin, County Kerry + 353 66 9762357 www.solysombra.ie. Open dinner.*

Zest Café
Nicola Foley's Zest Café is a pulsing and integral part of the Foley family's trio of establishments, a stylish and happening room where it seems that every dish they offer, from breakfast to brunch to lunch and into the afternoon, somehow has your name on it. Value and service chime sweetly with every other detail of a café that gives us zest for living. *School Road, Killorglin, County Kerry + 353 66 979 0303 www.zestcafe. ie. Open day time.*

Jack's
The shelves here are groaning with breads, cakes and superb deli foods. *Lower Bridge Street, Killorglin, County Kerry + 353 66 976 1132. Open day time.*

Jack's Coastguard Restaurant

Jack's is an icon in and around Cromane, a sure-fire success story for beautifully cooked seafood served in a lovely room with a superlative location. The Keary family really do their best to look after everyone. *Cromane, County Kerry + 353 66 9769102 www.jackscromane.com. Open lunch and dinner.*

Petit Delice

You don't really expect to find a French bakery and tea rooms on the Ring of Kerry, but here it is: Petit Delice is bakery, lunch time destination, ice cream stop, chocolate fix and coffee stop! 'You can imagine that you are deep in La France Profonde', said the *FT*. There is a second branch in Killarney. *Cahirciveen, County Kerry + 353 87 9903572*

O'Neill's The Point Bar

Michael and Bridie O'Neill source their fish from Quinlan's fish shops for their fish and shellfish menu, and the cooking is lip smackin' simple and tasty. Make sure to get here early – it's a very busy spot – to enjoy spankingly fresh seafood in a charming, family-run pub. *Renard Point, Cahirciveen, County Kerry + 353 66 9472165 Open lunch & dinner in season.*

QCs

Kate and Andrew Cooke added the most stunningly stylish series of rooms to their fine restaurant a few years back, and instantly established QC's as the hippest destination on the Ring of Kerry. Eddie Gannon's cooking in the restaurant follows the design ethos of QC's: take top-class materials, and treat them with empathy and respect, imagination and creativity. *3 Main Street, Cahirciveen, County Kerry + 353 66 9472244 www.qcbar.com. Open lunch and dinner.*

Local Food

Sneem Black Pudding

Sneem is a tiny village which manages to boast not just one handmade Kerry black pudding, but two. You will find them in O'Sullivan's butcher's, and in Burns' family butcher's. Buy both to compare and contrast, and remember that black pudding is cooked and is best if heated in the oven, rather than fried in a frying pan.

The Moorings

Pan-fried hake with Gubbeen chorizo mash and lemon butter. Now, isn't that just the sort of lip smackin' dinner dish that the hungry traveller wants to find set before him, after a long day's journeying out and back to the Skelligs? Indeed it is, and it's just the sort of thing Patricia and Gerard will set before you in The Moorings. Mr and Mrs Kennedy have made the Moorings a little world unto itself, with the restaurant, bar, gift shop, guest rooms and a self-catering cottage. *Portmagee, County Kerry + 353 66 9477108 Open lunch & dinner.*

Iskeroon

Iskeroon's extraordinary location at the ocean's edge explains its world-wide renown as an amazing place to stay, and David and Geraldine have designed and furnished their suites and self-catering apartment with exactly the right sort of chic rusticity. Iskeroon is pretty unforgettable, pretty amazing, not least the drive down the winding road and then across the beach to the house. *Caherdaniel, County Kerry + 353 66 9475119 www.iskeroon.com.*

The Boathouse

This stylish waterside restaurant is owned and run by the smart people behind The Park Hotel, Kenmare. A pretty relaxed space, only yards from the sea. *Drom-quinna Estate, Kenmare, County Kerry + 353 64 6642889 Open lunch and dinner.*

Brook Lane
The Brook Lane is a boutique hotel that offers exactly what you want, without pretension, without silliness, without nonsense. Despite their relative youth, Dermot and Una have mature heads on their shoulders, and we love the way they do their thing. *Kenmare, County Kerry + 353 64 6642077 www.brooklanehotel.com.*

Hawthorn House
Mary and Noel run a cosy, comfy, welcoming B&B right in the centre of Kenmare, and it's a perfect base for exploring the culinary charms of Kenmare and for relaxing after a day on the WAW. *Shelbourne Street, Kenmare, County Kerry + 353 64 6641035.*

Jam
The staff in Jam, a comfy, cosy café are so good, so charming, so friendly, that were they to tell us that they had nothing but cheese strings and gruel to offer, we would sit down and have cheese strings and gruel. Thankfully, they offer smashing proper food, and the place is always packed. *6 Henry Street, Kenmare, County Kerry + 353 64 6641591. Open day time.*

Virginia's Guesthouse
Kenmare is based around a pretty triangle of streets, and this comfort-focused guesthouse is right in the heart of it. Their breakfasts are only famous. *Henry Street, Kenmare, County Kerry + 353 86 3720625*

Above: Mulcahy's Restaurant
Below: The Park Hotel

Mulcahy's

Quietly, surely, confidently, whilst everyone was looking somewhere else, Bruce Mulcahy climbed to the top of the culinary tree in Ireland. It's where he belongs, and his confidence today means he inhabits the lofty space comfortably, rubbing shoulders with the best. His cooking is vivid and fun: his veal cheek ravioli would thrill you if you ate it in a Ligurian enoteca. His beef tartare with tarragon purée and toasted sourdough would make Fernand Point smile, before M. Point wolfed down the plate. The attention to detail is microscopic, the success is massive. Great value for money, too. *Henry Street, Kenmare, County Kerry + 353 64 6642383. Open dinner.*

No 35

Dermot and Una Brennan run restaurant No 35 as well as the lovely Brook Lane Hotel, and you will see the same fastidious creativity here in the centre of town in a charming restaurant. The food sourcing is meticulous and in particular don't miss their own rare-breed pork. *Main Street, Kenmare, County Kerry + 353 64 6641559. Open dinner.*

Packie's

Martin Hallisey's cooking in Packie's, one of the legendary Kenmare addresses, is neither modern nor traditional, though it has elements of both. Truthfully, it's food that is outside of fashion, and outside of time, so you might have roast duck, or Irish stew, or cod Provencale or seafood sausage with beurre blanc and it will all be delicious. Service is as genial as the chef and his food. One of the Kenmare standard bearers. *Henry Street, Kenmare, County Kerry + 353 64 6641508. Open dinner.*

Park Hotel

If you think that polished, practiced hospitality has little or no place in our modern, informal world, then come to Francis and John Brennan's legendary hotel, The Park, and you will find that polished, practiced hospitality is alive and well. What's more, you will discover that doing things correctly is infinitely pleasing, and that it is in no way anachronistic in our modern, informal world. Hospitality this good exists outside of time or fashion. *Kenmare, County Kerry + 353 64 664 1200 www.parkkenmare.com*

Purple Heather

Grainne O'Connell is one of the select band of Kenmare Food Heroes, people who not only carved out the town's reputation for good food, but who also maintain it, day after day, through sheer hard work. Something about the room always makes us yearn for classic food when we are here – chicken liver pâté with Cumberland sauce, the mushroom omelette, the cheese platter, the seafood pie. Class. *Henry Street, Kenmare, County Kerry + 353 64 6641016*

Shelburne Lodge

Shelburne Lodge is one of the most beautiful places to stay in Ireland. Having distinguished herself as one of Kenmare's greatest cooks when she ran restaurants down in the town, in Shelburne Maura Foley shows herself to be one of the great designers, decorators, and hosts. Shelburne Lodge is sublime in every detail: the design, the decoration, the artworks and – most especially – the breakfasts, which are the stuff of legend.

Tom looks after everyone as if he was your favourite uncle. *Killowen, Kenmare, County Kerry + 353 64 6641013 www.shelburnelodge.com*

Opposite & Centre: Mulcahy's Restaurant

Opposite: Shelburne Lodge flowers

Local Food

Kerry boasts a number of small chocolate factories in unlikely locations. Way out in Ballinskelligs you will find the **Skelligs Chocolate Company** beside the **Cocoa Bean Artisan Chocolates.** These two gifted artisan chocolate companies work side-by-side at St Finian's Bay. You are welcome to visit the factory, they give regular tours.

Meanwhile further inland, French chocolatier Benoit Lorge works out of an old post office by the side of the road in Bonane making the prized **Lorge Chocolates.**

www.skelligschocolate.com
www.lorgechocolate.com

Truffle Pig

There is both excellent food and an excellent atmosphere in the Truffle Pig, so it's a great coffee and cake destination in the morning or afternoon, it's an excellent lunchtime destination – do try their very good pies – and there is nice food-to-go if you are heading off on the WAW. *Henry Street, Kenmare, County Kerry + 353 64 6642953.*

Vanilla Grape

Alain Bras stocks an idiosyncratic, intriguing selection of wines in this cute shop. Originally a sommelier and wine lecturer of considerable renown, M. Bras culls wines from 35 regions for his shelves, and the selection is distinguished by his in-depth knowledge of the entire world of wine. *12 Henry Street, Kenmare, County Kerry + 353 64 6640694 www.alainbras.com.*

Wharton's

There are droves of people who will argue vehemently with you should you dare to suggest that there is a better chipper than Wharton's of Kenmare. They will be joined by the massed citizens of Kenmare, who cherish their famous fish and chip shop, a place where everything is made from scratch and cooked to order. Ace grub, and smashing staff. *Main Street, Kenmare, County Kerry + 353 64 6642622 www.whartonskenmare.com. Open lunch and dinner.*

Josie's Lakeview House Restaurant

Josie's is the last stop in County Kerry and here you will find simple cooking, terrific views of Glanmore Lake, a bed and breakfast apartment and even a self-catering cottage if you feel like getting to know the area better. The lunchtime offer is soups, salads and sandwiches, with a more extensive assortment of fish dishes and rack of lamb and steaks in the evening, and plenty of good vegetables. It's fun, it's remote, and there is generosity evident everywhere. *Lauragh, County Kerry + 353 64 6683155 www.josiesrestaurant.ie Open lunch and dinner.*

11
The Ring
of Beara

The Beara Peninsula is where Irish artisan food production was reignited. Sometime around about 1976, way down south on the rugged Beara, in farthest, deepest West Cork, Veronica and Norman Steele, who had three cows on their little farm, "started making cheese as a way of stashing milk for the winter".

WILD ATLANTIC WAY

The Steeles called their cheese Milleens, and it was a washed-rind, semi-soft cheese made with raw milk. Those were the only aspects of Milleens that were conventional, however. In terms of flavour and texture, Milleens was unlike anything being made by anyone else anywhere else. Milleens was a mighty template of tastes, with floral, sweet, mushroomy, resinous flavour notes all bundled up in its carefully, hand-washed rind.

It was a cheese that was both earthy and ethereal, and it created the signature style for all the Irish farmhouse cheeses that quickly followed its example: when your cheese expressed the singular place from which it originated, then you had made a successful cheese.

Milleens spoke of West Cork. It spoke of Beara, of the cow in the field on the sea-surrounded peninsula.

Local Food

'It's basically a recipe' says Michael O'Neill on the process of making **Irish Atlantic Sea Salt.** The O'Neills create crisp flakes of snow-white salt that are slightly moist, flaky and crumble nicely when you crush them between your fingers. This is an artisan ingredient that has seen no refinement or additives, and consequently is a treasure of the region, with its own special taste.

www.irishatlanticsalt.ie

Harrington's
Come to Harrington's to enjoy a coffee in the café in the morning or a sandwich at lunchtime, sit outside at a table in the summer sunshine, then choose a nice bottle of wine to bring home for dinner. Harrington's is an axis of good things, the centre of the universe brought down to the Beara. *Ardgroom, County Cork + 353 27 74003. Open day time until early evening.*

Auntie May's
Auntie May's, in beautiful Eyeries, serves delicious food, and it's a real must-stop! destination on Beara. The cooking is simple and true — excellent Santa Barbara fish stew; tasty burgers; properly-made sandwiches; nice smoked salmon. The room is atmospheric, service is relaxed and friendly. *Main Street, Eyeries, County Cork + 353 27 74477. Open lunch and dinner.*

Dursey Deli
The Dursey Deli is the original food cart! The Dursey Deli is essentially a chipper on wheels, but if you're lucky there'll be fresh mackerel from Dursey's beautiful bay. Time your trip on the cable car to coincide with lunch, and keep your fingers crossed for that mackerel. *Dursey, County Cork + 353 86 1799270. Open day time, seasonally.*

Copper Kettle
The Copper Kettle is a modest space, specialising in enormous breakfasts. The CK is much beloved of the strange and wonderful inhabitants of the Beara Peninsula, who come here to meet, drink coffee and read the *Examiner. Castletownbere, County Cork + 353 27 71792. Open day time.*

Loop de Loop
A key stop in Castletownbere, this handsome eco emporium sells wholesome foods. Don't pass through Castletown without calling in. *Bank Place, Castletownbere, County Cork + 353 27 70770*

McCarthy's Bar

As you sip a pint in the legendary McCarthy's Bar, make sure to ask Adrienne the story of her father Aidan's life. She will refer you to Aidan's book, which tells the incredible story of his wartime service. Once you open it, you won't be able to put it down. The McCarthys are special, and McCarthy's Bar is special. 'It might just be the

best pub in the world', wrote the late Pete McCarthy. Too right. *The Square, Castletownbere, County Cork + 353 27 70014. Food served day time.*

Taste

Sheila Power's shop is simply jammers with good things — brilliant breads, organic vegetables, coffee, cheeses, wholefoods, wines, whatever you might need or could need. Nice sandwiches and wraps too, to take care of the hunger pangs. *Bank Place, Castletownbere, County Cork + 353 27 71943.*

Peg's Shop

Maureen Sullivan runs a lovely shop here in Peg's. Like the best Beara stores, it's friendly, atmospheric and fun, with lots of tasty things to eat and good bottles of wine. *Adrigole, County Cork + 353 27 60007.*

12
Bantry Bay to the Sheep's Head

The Sheep's Head peninsula has always been the sleeper peninsula in West Cork, not as well-known as the Mizen, often overlooked in favour of the Beara. But a quiet renaissance has been taking place here in recent times, spurred initially by the Sheep's Head Way – which actually runs, or should we say, walks, all the way to Gougane Barra – and by the collective actions of the Sheep's Head producers group.

Today there is a critical cluster of food people and food places on the peninsula, unified by high standards and a creative imagination. And if you are persuaded to stay and linger awhile whilst travelling the WAW, by the B&B's and restaurants, then you will discover a very special, very quiet place, a place for walking, cycling, swimming, hiking. The Sheep's Head is a place that seems to attract unlikely people, who then do unlikely things there. And the great exemplar in this regard is Jeffa Gill, who has made Durrus Farmhouse Cheese, way, way up at the top of the hill of Coomken, for more than thirty years. We don't know if Ms Gill ever asked an accountant if it was a good business idea to make a raw milk cheese at the top of a remote hill on a remote peninsula: we suspect she didn't.

WILD
ATLANTIC
WAY

Opposite: Good Things Café

Local Food

West Cork is the home of Irish farmhouse cheese, with the pioneering semi-soft cheeses from **Milleens, Durrus** and **Gubbeen,** all of them pioneer cheeses, and all of them made by mighty women – Veronica Steele, Jeffa Gill, and Giana Ferguson. Someone needs to write that Ph.D thesis on what these women have achieved for Irish food, and for Irish feminism, and for Irish farming.

Manning's Emporium

Who would have thought that Manning's Emporium could be so wonderfully rejuvenated at this stage of its existence? The touchpaper was lit by the arrival of Val's niece, Laura, and her husband Andrew Heath into the business and their enthusiasm and energy has sprinkled the whole enterprise with some magic dust. More than just an emporium for the finest locally sourced food in the area, Manning's is now a super cool café – it might be the only place in West Cork serving a Flat White – and just try those raspberry cupcakes or scones – the food is delicious. The genius touch is the addition of a sherry bar, right at the front of the shop. It's hard to imagine anything more enjoyable than sitting at that little bar with a glass of chilled fino sherry, some local cheese or cured meats, listening to the genial and venerable Val chatting away to customers and so visibly enjoying his work. A priceless slice of West Cork. *Ballylickey, County Cork + 353 27 50456 www.manningsemporium.ie. Open day time.*

Sea View House Hotel

Kathleen O'Sullivan's beautiful hotel in Ballylickey is the favourite West Cork destination for very many very discriminating people. Ms O'Sullivan runs her hotel the old school way, with correct cooking, correct service, simple and correct design, eager and correct housekeeping. As a guest, the pleasures to be derived from her didactic approach to running an hotel are myriad, and you find yourself saying 'Why aren't there more hotels like this, places where nothing is too much trouble, places where they look after you? ' And look after you is what they do in the Sea View House Hotel. *Ballylickey, County Cork + 353 27 50073 www.seaviewhousehotel.com*

Bay View

The Bay View is a valuable stop both for its pretty tea rooms and also for some stylish accommodation, just south of Glengarriff. *Reenmeen, Glengarriff, County Cork + 353 27 63030 www.thebayviewboutique-guesthouse.com. Cafe open day time.*

Bantry Market

You will find us in Bantry Market on Friday mornings, hunting down the Toonsbridge burrata, the Maughnasilly eggs, the Wok About stir-fries, the organic vegetables and the Gubbeen pork, the West Cork pies and the O'Driscoll's fish, before we have a slice of Base pizza or maybe something tasty from Frankie's BBQ. *Wolfe Tone Square, Bantry, County Cork. Fridays.*

Below: Martin O'Flynn, Maughnasily Farm, in the Bantry Market

Eden Crest

Josephine's pretty, flower-bedecked B&B is just a short walk from Bantry town, and as well as very cosy accommodation and excellent breakfasts from the proprietor, there is also a self-catering cottage available right next door. *Glengarriff Road, Bantry, County Cork + 353 27 51110 www.bantrybandb.com*

Above: The Snug
Opposite: The Stuffed Olive

Fish Kitchen

Ann Marie's Fish Kitchen is upstairs above the fish shop, and it's a charming room in which to enjoy excellent fish cookery right in the centre of Bantry. Great service, and excellent value for money, means that the Fish Kitchen really ticks all the boxes. *New Street, Bantry, County Cork + 353 27 56651 www.thefishkitchen.ie. Open lunch and dinner.*

Organico

Hannah and Rachel Dare and their team run one of the classic destinations in West Cork. Organico is the best wholefood store imaginable, and it is also the most wonderful café with inspired cooking. They have a great bakery, great daytime cooking, and together the shop and café are a vital address which has all you need. And they are always getting better, and better. *Glengarriff Road, Bantry, County Cork + 353 27 51391 www.organico.ie. Open day time.*

The Snug

The Snug isn't trendy. It's a classic traditional West Cork pub, and that is precisely what everyone likes about it. Maurice and Colette take care of things; he cooks, she minds the bar and the customers, and they both do a superb job. So, pull up a stool at the counter and order plaice with mushroom sauce, a good cheese burger, West Cork sirloin and gravy, baked haddock, minute steak, and relish the amazing vegetables. Heartwarming, delicious and delightful, and sure let's have another pint, what do you say? *The Quay, Bantry, County Cork + 353 27 50057. Open lunch and dinner.*

Stuffed Olive

Here's the kind of cook Trish Messom of The Stuffed Olive is: when she makes a Portuguese custard tart, she will make a better Portuguese custard tart than they make in Lisbon. Really.

She makes a trifle that looks like it just walked out of a Janet and Allan Ahlberg children's story. You look at it and say to yourself: this doesn't belong on a shelf, this belongs in a dream!

Ms Messon's cookery is dreamy, and dream like. She is one of those rare cooks whose every culinary gesture creates an archetype. Her cakes are dreamscapes. Her savoury cooking is ruddy and real. Her salads shout: goodness! Her drinks are narcotic. Her traditional lamb stew would sustain the nation. All this, and you also get terrific service from Trish's daughters, Sarah and Grace, and the sort of vivid, vibrant ambience in the room that pulls you in off the street. A true star of Bantry, no doubt about it. *Bridge Street, Bantry, County Cork + 353 27 55883. Open day time.*

Bank House Restaurant on Whiddy Island
Staying here is both restorative and exciting, from quiet freshwater fishing to adventurous sea fishing. The family run the local ferry and do their very best to offer a memorable holiday. *Whiddy Island, County Cork + 353 86 8626734 www.whiddyferry.com*

Drumcloc House B&B
Swim or fish from their shoreline at Drumcloc, and enjoy good West Cork hospitality. There is a tennis court and a peaceful garden, so you can choose to be active, or not. *Bantry, County Cork + 353 27 50030 www. dromclochouse.com.*

Sheep's Head Producers Shop Restaurant & Market
West Cork is known to be a place where artists, crafts people and food lovers have chosen to live, and that's what makes this collaborative enterprise so special. There is a shop, selling local foods, a regular market, and, as we go to press, a new restaurant. It's exciting, and it's terrific fun, so come along and meet everyone. *The Old Creamery, Kilcrohane, County Cork + 353 86 303 0991 livingthesheepsheadway.com*

The Tin Pub
The Tin Pub is a legendary bar just on the edge of Ahakista village, with amiable locals and lots of good music. *Ahakista, County Cork + 353 27 67203*

Heron Gallery & Café
Annabel Langrish has a funky café alongside her beautiful gallery, where she sells her paintings, ceramics and crafts, along with the work of other artists. If you can leave without buying an artwork you are indeed made of stern stuff. *Ahakista, County Cork + 353 27 67278 www.annabellangrish.ie. Open day time.*

Arundel's by the Pier
Shane and Fiona's bar and restaurant has a drop-dead gorgeous location, and to enjoy something delicious sitting outside at the water's edge on a sunny West

Cork day is an experience that is hard to beat. They serve bar food downstairs, whilst the restaurant is upstairs above the bar. There are good local mussels, there are Durrus farmhouse cheese fritters and that celebrated local food hero might turn up served with smoked haddock and baby potatoes. There is Dingle crab meat in a gratin, and cod with a herb crust, and the service and value are excellent. *Ahakista, County Cork + 353 27 67033. Open lunch and dinner.*

Above: Durrus Village

Gallan Mor

Lorna and Noel's B&B is a modern, purpose-built house, but the Burkes have smartly created a new house from the old West Cork architectural vernacular, so it reads new, but feels nice and old. The house is colourful, the rooms are swaddling in their comfort and their crafty utility, and the views out across Dunmanus Bay are eye-wipingly wonderful. There is also an excellent self-catering cottage. *Kealties, Durrus, County Cork + 353 27 62732 www.gallanmor.com*

Good Things Café

Carmel Somers is one of the most imaginative and creative cooks in all of Ireland, and Good Things is an iconic destination, as you will understand when you see all the famous people who come here to eat Ms Somer's unique food. The Durrus cheese and spinach pizza is unlike anything you have ever eaten, and everything else on the menu is just as unpredictable, save for being predictably delicious. Ms Somers also runs very highly regarded cookery classes. *Durrus, County Cork + 353 27 51426 www.thegoodthingscafe.com. Open lunch and dinner seasonally.*

Blair's Cove

The setting of Blair's Cove, jutting out into Dunmanus Bay, will take your breath away when you arrive here. The cathedral-like dining room is also utterly gorgeous, and there are some fine rooms in and around the courtyard where you can stay. *Durrus, County Cork + 353 27 61127 www.blairscove.ie. Open dinner.*

Above: Good Things
Opposite: Arundel's Pub

13
Goleen,
Mizen Head and
Roaring Water Bay

Mizen Head is where things end, so they say. If you travel from one end of Ireland to the other, then you will have gone "from Malin Head to Mizen Head" to quote the phrase. We suspect that for many travellers on the WAW, Mizen will be one of the key end-of-the-country places to make sure you get to, to make sure you tick off on the itinerary, so you can say that you climbed the 99 steps and crossed the bridge.

**WILD
ATLANTIC
WAY**

But the real reason to come to Mizen Head is not just to say you've been, instead it is to experience the exhilarating atmosphere in a place where the air seems super-charged, powered by sea salt and mighty winds, by the glint of the sunshine on the sea, by the sense of separateness, the place apart.

You feel very small indeed when in this environment, you feel very fragile next to the power of the sea and the elements in their most elemental glory. And yet, when you reflect on the lives that were lived by the signal men who used to man the lighthouse, then you also appreciate the power of the human spirit, the power to withstand isolation, the power to confront the elements, the human will to shine a light into the darkness.

Fortview House
Here's what people say about Violet Connell's famous B&B: 'Probably the best B&B we have ever stayed in. Violet Connell is one of the nicest people you will ever meet and we loved every minute staying in this smashing house.' No more need be said about wonderful Fortview. *Gurtyowen, Toormore, Goleen, County Cork + 353 28 35324 www.fortviewhousegoleen.com.*

The Crookhaven Inn
Emma and Freddy serve smashing food in the Crookhaven Inn, and they do it calmly and don't make a fuss about it. The signature dishes are resoundingly successful – braised lamb shank with rosemary mash; fish soup with aioli; rigatoni with roasted red pepper pesto and smoked chicken; monkfish wrapped in Gubbeen pancetta. After a day at Barleycove beach, it's bliss. *Crookhaven, County Cork + 353 28 35309 www.crookhaveninn.com. Open lunch and dinner.*

O'Sullivan's Bar
The O'Sullivan family's bar is as much a part of West Cork as pastel-painted villages and the Fastnet Rock. You come here to this unique bar to chill, to have excellent sandwiches and chowder, and to see who else has come here to chill and have excellent sandwiches and chowder. *Crookhaven, County Cork + 353 28 35319 www.osullivanscrookhaven.ie. Open lunch and early evening.*

Mizen Head Visitor's Centre
You can get a cup of tea, a toasted sandwich, or bowl of seafood chowder in the Mizen Head Centre, when visiting the Mizen Head Signal Station. *Mizen Head, County Cork + 353 28 35115 www.mizenhead.net Open day time.*

Grove House

Katarina and Nico run Schull's best place to stay, and they also run Schull's best place to eat, thanks to Nico's fun, smart cooking. The ingredients are well sourced and Nico handles them with skill and flair. Value for money is really exceptional, and Katarina's warm welcome means everyone is very chilled from the moment they walk in the door. *Colla Road, Schull, County Cork + 353 28 28067 www.grovehouseschull. com. Open lunch and dinner. Booking essential.*

Hackett's

The grooviest bar in Schull has great drinks and brilliant craic along with some really punky, funky cooking – you won't get a better bowl of soup in West Cork than the Hackett's signature soups. *Main Street, Schull, County Cork + 353 28 28625. Open lunch and Fri & Saturday nights if pre booked.*

Casa Diego

Diego and his friends make nice Spanish-accented food here at the top of Main Street. The lean rooms suit the simple elegance of the food, and it's a splendid place to feed children on good patatas bravas, paella, calamari, albondigas and their very good homemade croquettes. *Main Street, Schull, County Cork + 353 86 3978364 www.casadiego.ie. Open lunch and dinner.*

Antonio's

Antonio's is one of the busiest restaurants in West Cork, and its charismatic mix of good Italian food and good pizzas is a winning formula. Their signature pasta dishes are really fine, and an evening here is great theatre and great fun. *Main Street, Ballydehob, County Cork + 353 28 37139 Open lunch and dinner.*

Schull Sunday Market

Schull Market is one of the best of the West Cork markets, always dotted with great food offerings that make for a special Sunday lunch.

Hudson's

The artisan producers of West Cork beat a path to Hudson's with their produce, closely followed by Gillian Hudson's devoted customers who want to get their hands on all that lovely produce. The combination of a fine bakery, a wholefood store, a vegetable shop and a fine café makes for a one-stop-oasis of good things. *Main Street, Ballydehob, County Cork + 353 28 37565 www.hudsonswholefood.com. Open day time.*

Above: Antonio's
Below: Thornton's Organics
Opposite: Field's Supermarket

West Cork Gourmet Store

Joanne has created a clever and enduring concept in this tiny space. Food is prepared behind a large display of charcuterie and salads; chairs are dotted around underneath shelves of oriental and Irish produce, and there is a tiny garden out back. WCGS is a place for lunch, and the occasional summer dinner. *Staball Hill, Ballydehob, County Cork + 353 28 25991 Open daily.*

Bridge House

Mona Best runs the most idiosyncratic B&B in West Cork, and Ms Best is one of the great hostesses. *Bridge Street, Skibbereen, County Cork + 353 28 21273 www.bridgehouseskibbereen.com.*

Fields of Skibbereen

John Field's supermarket is one of the greatest food stores in Europe, and every good thing that is produced in West Cork can be found here, sold with knowledge and pride by a wonderful team of people. There is also a lovely tea room for breakfast and lunch, so don't miss this West Cork classic. *Main Street, Skibbereen, County Cork + 353 28 21400 www.fieldsofskibbereen.ie Open daily.*

Kalbo's

Siobhan O'Callaghan is one of the best cooks in West Cork, and everything cooked in Kalbo's has her signature of superb sourcing, and sophisticated cooking. And the chocolate brownies are the best. *48 North Street, Skibbereen, County Cork + 353 28 21515. Open daily and dinner Fri-Sat.*

La Concha

Fred Perez has a neat little operation here in La Concha, with tapas slates to share, and then grilled fresh fish with a little butter. Nice, and simple. *72 Bridge Street, Skibbereen, County Cork + 353 28 23436 www.laconcha.ie. Open lunch and dinner.*

Liss Ard Estate

Liss Ard is an impossibly beautiful place to stay and eat, and don't miss both the beautiful gardens and sky garden designed by the great James Turrell. *Russagh, Skibbereen, County Cork + 353 28 4000 www.lissard-estate.com*

West Cork Hotel

Chef Christian Pozimski and his team conjure up tasty cooking in the venerable WCH, one of the singular landmarks of West Cork. Excellent staff make for a very fine place to stay and eat when on the WAW. *Ilen Street, Skibbereen, County Cork + 353 28 21277 www.westcorkhotel.com*

The Islands of West Cork

Legend has it there are 1,000 islands in Roaring Water Bay. Whilst you can take this with a pinch of salt, do be sure to take the ferry over to one of the larger islands, where you will enjoy not just their unique characters but some great food with wonderful people making it special.

Island Cottage, Heir Island www.islandcottage.com
Séan Rua's Restaurant and Shop, North Harbour, Cape Clear
The Islander's Rest & Murphy's Pub, Sherkin Island www.sherkin.ie

'Suddenly an entire galaxy of stars explodes from my fingertips, sending fading constellations of pale blue lights swirling out into the black'.

That's the travel writer Kevin Rushby, writing in *The Guardian*, about one of the most magical things that you can do when in and around this part of the WAW: take a night-time kayak trip, in order to have a galaxy of stars explode from your fingertips.

Or, to put it a little more scientifically, take the trip and discover the mesmerising magic that is bioluminescence: see what happens when microscopic phytoplankton release their stored-up light energy when they come into contact with your kayak paddle, or with your hand.

And that's not all you might see on a night trip. Whilst the bioluminescence accounts for the starlight in the sea, the stars overhead are magically clear and crystal-like, something that is often an incredible discovery for city dwellers, who never experience clear skies on account of street lighting. Stars above, and stars below, star-filled and bible black, and the whole experience is utterly mesmerising. 'The magical nocturnal world' is how Mr Rushby describes it.

Inis Beg

The Boathouse at Inish Beg is one of the best known, and one of the most beautiful, places to stay anywhere in Ireland. But even if you can't bag the Boathouse, all the houses on this brilliant estate are cherishable. *Inis Beg, Baltimore, County Cork + 353 28 21745 www. inishbeg.com*

Glebe Gardens

The Perry family are superlative gardeners, which means that the ingredients they cook with in the restaurant in Glebe have travelled only yards to your plate. And don't miss that lemon meringue cake!
Baltimore, County Cork + 353 28 20232 www.glebe-gardens.com. Open day time.

Rolf's

Johannes and Frederike have an excellent restaurant and excellent rooms in this lively and unpretentious hostelry. It's characterful and fun, and the cooking brings in the locals as well as visitors to Baltimore.
Baltimore, County Cork + 353 28 20289 www. rolfscountryhouse.eu

Slipway

Wilmie Owen runs a pretty and winning B&B just across the road from the sea at beautiful Baltimore. *The Cove, Baltimore, County Cork + 353 28 20134 www.theslipway.com*

Above (top and middle):
Glebe Gardens

Mary's Ann's Bar

A justly celebrated and very commodious bar and restaurant in lovely little Castletownshend, the village with a tree in the middle of the road. *Castletownshend, County Cork + 353 28 36146*

The Celtic Ross Hotel

The Wycherley family's hotel is right by the side of the N71, and just outside Rosscarbery village itself. It's a professional and pristine operation. *Rosscarbery, County Cork + 353 23 8848722 www.celticrosshotel.com.*

O'Callaghan-Walsh

Martina and Sean cook and serve the best West Cork fish, and their scampi – and their mashed potato – are the stuff of legend. Sean is also one of the wittiest hosts in history, so you get a great sense of humour along with inspired fish cookery. *The Square, Rosscarbery, County Cork + 353 23 8848125. Open dinner*

Lis-Ardagh Lodge

Carol and Jim's Lis-Ardagh Lodge is the first choice for very many visitors to West Cork, and you will meet other guests here who have returned to the house on numerous occasions over the years. In addition to the B&B there are two self-catering apartments. *Union Hall, County Cork + 353 28 34951 www.lis-ardaghlodge.com.*

The Coffee Shop

Everyone comes to Carol Noonan's Coffee Shop in Union Hall, starting with breakfast, then on into lunch, and then for tea and cake in the afternoon. Pretty magical, especially if you have an appetite after a coastal walk or some sea kayaking. *Main Street, Union Hall, County Cork + 353 28 34444. Open daily.*

Above: Kayak seaweed safaris and night paddling (see page 149) with www.atlanticseakayaking.com

Galley Head Lighthouse

If you have never stayed in a lighthouse before, then try to book the keeper's cottages at Galley Head, and you will have an unforgettable experience. Everything that happens in the Lightkeeper's cottages takes place under that beam of light from the lighthouse, which sweeps rhythmically and powerfully, creating an unforgettable atmosphere that seems to bring an extra consciousness to everyday experiences. *Galley Head, County Cork www.irishlandmark.com*

Deasy's Harbour Bar

Caitlin Ruth has made the beautiful Deasy's – an atmospheric old inn in little Ring, just outside Clonakilty – into one of the most highly regarded restaurants in Ireland. Her cooking is like no other, and the poise and generosity of the dishes show a cook at her peak: white bean, Parmesan and rosemary soup; Sally Barnes' smoked mackerel with tomato and caper salad; incredible carrot mustard with duck rillettes and pickled raisins; crab claws with a lime, chilli and coriander butter; roasted squash with Toonsbridge mozzarella and herb croutons. Ms Ruth's cooking is amongst the very best, and no one is better at showcasing exceptional West Cork ingredients, and you will remember every bite as you travel the length of the WAW. *Ring Village, Clonakilty, County Cork + 353 23 8835741. Open dinner and weekend lunch.*

Below: Deasy's

Hart's

Aileen Hart runs one of the glories of Clon, a beautiful tea rooms with hip, adroit food that shines with care, sympathy and astuteness. Delightful, and a key element of this sweet town. *Ashe Street, Clonakilty, County Cork + 353 23 8835583. Open daily.*

Inchydoney

Owner Des O'Dowd and his team are rewriting the book of expectations at this fine beachside hotel, and they have one of the best, most committed crews working together that we have seen in recent times. The hotel seems to us to have matured beautifully, so that every element works compatibly, and it all adds up to a very special getaway in a very special setting. The beach outside is surfer paradise. *Clonakilty, County Cork + 353 23 8833143 www.inchydoneyisland.com*

Lettercollum Kitchen Project

For our money, Con and Karin and their team in Lettercollum Kitchen make the best pastry you can find in West Cork. Their quiches, their sausage rolls, their pies, are culinary poetry. So, if you are picnicking on the West Cork beaches, this is your first port of call, and when passing through town, it's a brilliant lunch stop. Lots of lovely things on the shelves, too. *22 Connolly Street, Clonakilty, County Cork + 353 23 8836938 www.lettercollum.ie. Open day time.*

Richy's Bar & Bistro

Richy's is a fine local bar and bistro which has served Clonakilty faithfully for a dozen years now, and it's a very child-friendly place. *4 Wolfe Tone Street, Clonakilty, County Cork + 353 23 8821852 www.richysbarandbistro.com. Open lunch and dinner.*

Scally's SuperValu

Eugene Scally's SuperValu is one of the supreme Irish supermarkets, distinguished by the range of superb West Cork foods, and by really great service. *Six Bridge, Clonakilty, County Cork + 353 23 8833088 www.supervaluclon.ie*

15
The Old Head
of Kinsale

The Old Head of Kinsale is marked on a map of the world produced by the Egyptian, Ptolemy, in the middle of the first century A.D., according to Allanah Hopkins' book *Eating Scenery: West Cork, The People & The Place*.

It is believed the information about the Old Head, and Cork city, the River Lee and Mizen Head which are also shown on the map, was given by sailors returning to the Mediterranean who had sailed the south west coast of Ireland. The Wild Atlantic Way has, then, been attracting visitors for millennia.

Elsewhere in her fine book, Ms Gallagher writes: 'When I first discovered the coast of West Cork, I thought I had found paradise, like many others before me. It seemed to be a place of infinite delights, where time had stood still, waiting for me to come along and explore.'

Many visitors experience this feeling, one of discovery, belonging and enchantment. It is intoxicating, and can be life-changing: you may simply decide that this is the paradise where you want to live, and your old life elsewhere is shaken off, and you step into the place of infinite delights.

WILD
ATLANTIC
WAY

Opposite: Fishy Fishy

The Glen

If you get the chance to stay at The Glen, you will know that dealing in enchantment is what Guy and Diana do in this beautiful country house. You will know that they seem to hand out unforgettable moments and memories along with the breakfasts, along with their amazing afternoon teas. And years later, those memories will come flooding back, unbidden – the beauty of the house, the beauty of the gardens, the comfort, the welcome – and you, too, will be like the enchanted child, the cat who got the cream. The Glen gives the gift that keeps on giving. *Kilbrittain, County Cork + 353 23 8849862 www.glencountryhouse.com*

Diva Boutique Bakery Café & Deli

Shannen Keane runs Diva bakery, Diva café and Diva deli, and they are all excellent. Originally from Seattle, Ms Keane brings an American energy and relish to her work, and everything fizzes with flavour. One lunch we enjoyed here was that rare event: an utterly perfect meal that could not be faulted in any way, from the spicy lentil soup to the Mexican tortilla. The breads from the bakery are superlative, and the shop is jammed with deicious things, so you can put together a smashing picnic and head for the beach. *Main Street, Ballinspittle, County Cork + 353 21 4778465 www.divaboutiquebakery.com. Open day time.*

Glebe Country House

Glebe is a world-unto-itself. There are the gardens, and the gardens furnish the house with lots of things for breakfast and dinner; there are apartments for the entire family to stay; there are the rooms in the house. They cater for weddings, specialise in house parties, and cook delightful food for breakfast and dinner. *Ballinadee, Bandon, County Cork + 353 21 4778294 www.glebecountryhouse.ie*

Gort na Nain

Virtually everything Lucy cooks with in this vegetarian B&B comes straight from Ultan's acclaimed organic farm. It's their own honey, their own eggs, their own chutneys, breads, pastas, the whole nine yards. So, get your feet under the table with your fellow guests to enjoy baby aubergines stuffed with courgettes and toasted pine nuts; Puy lentil and garlic potatoes wrapped up in chard parcels; home-made rhubarb ripple ice cream. And then upstairs to a cosy bed. *Ballyherkin, Nohoval, County Cork + 353 21 4770647 www.gortnanain.com*

The Black Pig

The Black Pig is a rockin' winebar and café run by ex-Ely stalwarts Siobhan Waldron and Gavin Ryan. Both the foods and the wines they serve are impeccably sourced, so decide from the brilliant wine list what you would like to drink, then share a tapas platter to begin and then tuck into the main dish of the day. The Black Pig has been buzzing from day one, so call ahead to ensure your name is chalked on the board when you arrive. *Kinsale, County Cork + 353 21 477 4101. Open dinner.*

Blindgate House

Maeve Coakley's house is one of the great designer B&B's, in a quiet part of busy Kinsale. It's a really comfortable, stylish house and the breakfasts are particularly good. *Blindgate, Kinsale, County Cork + 353 21 4777858 www.blindgatehouse.com*

Opposite: Diva Boutique Bakery

Craft Brewery

Kinsale Porter
Sam and Maudeline Black brew a small range of beers in Kinsale, and you can see them at work when they conduct their brewery tours. They make a very fine Black IPA and a Kinsale Ale, and the newest arrival is The Session. There are also other beauties such as the draught-only Beoir #1, which comes in at a whopping 9%ABV.

Crackpots

Crackpots is first and foremost a restaurant, with some very nice cooking, but it is also a gallery, a ceramics workshop, a rental apartment, and Carole Norman also has a B&B just outside Kinsale. Phew! Ms Norman is a mighty powerhouse, so step in here and enjoy the energy and the fun. *Cork Street, Kinsale, County Cork + 353 21 4772847 www.crackpots. ie. Open lunch and dinner.*

Fishy Fishy

For first time visitors to Fishy Fishy, Martin Shanahan's cooking often comes as a revelation – fish can taste this delicious! this moreish! this sweet! Mr Shanahan's secret lies not merely with technique, but also with his inspired sourcing, whereby the fish comes straight in off the boats and straight into the kitchen, and then straight onto the plate: you simply can't eat fresher fish than you will enjoy in this thunderously busy seafood restaurant. *Crowley Quay, Kinsale, County Cork + 353 21 4700415 www.fishyfishy.ie*

The Lemon Leaf Café

Tracy Keoghan sources her ingredients carefully in this pretty café in the centre of Kinsale, so there are both nice foods on the shelves to buy and take away, and nice foods on the menu to order whilst you sit down and enjoy a charming room with a great vibe.
70 Main Street, Kinsale, County Cork + 353 21 4709792 www.lemonleafcafe.ie. Open day time.

Man Friday

Philip Horgan's Man Friday restaurant is one of the longest-established restaurants in Ireland, and is heading towards 40 years of service and 40 years of making people happy. It's classic cooking – deep-fried brie; sole on the bone; fillet steak with cream, brandy and peppercorns – and it's always welcome and fun, with great service. *Scilly, Kinsale, County Cork + 353 21 4772260 www.manfridaykinsale.ie. Open dinner.*

Max's Wine Bar

Anne Marie and Olivier Queyva describe their restaurant as being both 'quaint' and 'professional', and that is just right, though we should also add 'unpretentious' to the roll-call of flattering adjectives. Everything marries well in this delightful set of rooms – the food; the decor with its artful bricolage; the service, which is calm, confident, and charming. The Queyvas make it look easy, and that is part of the charm of this Kinsale institution. *48 Main Street, Kinsale, County Cork + 353 21 4772443 www.maxs.ie. Open dinner.*

Quay Food Co

An excellent wholefood and specialist shop, invaluable for collecting the ingredients for a good picnic. *Market Quay, Kinsale, County Cork + 353 21 4774000 www.quayfood.com. Open day time.*

Toddie's @ The Bulman

Happily housed in the classic bar space of the Bulman, Pearse O'Sullivan's cooking in Toddie's has never been better than it is right now, pulling in all of his international influences from a young life spent in both Trinidad and, ahem, Surrey: Trinidad-style crab gratin; Dublin Bay prawn soup with chilli, lemongrass and coriander; skewered chicken with wasabi coleslaw. *Summercove, Kinsale, County Cork + 353 21 4777769 www.toddies.ie. Open lunch & dinner.*

WILD ATLANTIC WAY
SLÍ AN ATLANTAIGH FHIÁIN

About the Wild Atlantic Way:

The Wild Atlantic Way is Ireland's first long-distance touring route, stretching from the Foyle Bridge in Derry, through the Inishowen Peninsula, and then travelling along the entire western coastline, ending 2,500km later, in Kinsale in County Cork.

The route is well-signposted throughout, and includes various loop routes and discovery points. Maps of the route are available on-line, and maps and more information about the route can be found from the Irish tourist board websites, including:
www.ireland.com/wild-atlantic-way.

About McKennas' Guides:

John and Sally McKenna have been publishing food and accommodation guides to Ireland for over twenty-five years, and have won local and international awards for their publications.

The publications include a range of digital options as well as this book on **Where to Eat and Stay on the Wild Atlantic Way.**

We publish *Smart Guides* to Irish food, restaurants and accommodation, for iPhones, tablets and smart phones. Look out for and download our The **100 Best Restaurants in Ireland 2014**. Look out also for our guide to The **100 Best Places to Stay in Ireland**, and also city guides and county guides, all describing the best places to eat, shop and stay. Forthcoming is a digital Smart Guide listing the best places to **Eat and Stay on the Wild Atlantic Way**.

www.guides.ie lists all the activities and publications connected with *McKennas' Guides*, and contains many recommendations for great places to eat and stay and wonderful local Irish foods. We also publish a **Who's Who** of Irish food. Other things that are published through the website include:

Megabites is a regular on-line digital magazine that you can subscribe to from the website www.guides.ie. Let us deliver it to your inbox, and it is free.

The Irish Food Channel is our independent video channel featuring people in food from all around the country.

We are on Facebook **www.facebook.com/ BridgestoneGuides** and **www.facebook.com/ wheretoeatandstayonthewildatlanticway** check here for updates on everything to do with the WAW.

We are on Twitter with **@McKennasGuides** and Instagram with **Sally McKenna.**